Bedside Companion for Food Lovers

Bedside Companion for Food Lovers

EDITED BY JANE MCMORLAND HUNTER

BATSFORD

First published in the United Kingdom in 2023 by
B. T. Batsford Ltd
43 Great Ormond Street
London
WC1N 3HZ

An imprint of B. T. Batsford Holdings Ltd

ISBN 978 1 84994 796 1

A CIP catalogue record for this book is available from the
British Library.

10 9 8 7 6 5 4 3 2 1

Reproduction by Rival Colour Ltd, UK
Printed and bound by Toppan Leefung Printing International Ltd,
China

Illustrations by Elen Winata

CONTENTS

For Sally,
and obviously for Matilda,
with all my love.

Acknowledgements

As always, a huge thank you to everyone at Hatchards for looking
after my books so well. I could not have compiled this anthology
without a great deal of help from friends, in particular, Sally Hughes
and Julie Apps. They suggested titles and researched entries for
me – for which, many thanks. My editor at Batsford, Nicola
Newman, makes compiling these anthologies a true pleasure.
As always Matilda, my small grey tabby cat, acts as paperweight on
anything I am trying to read, keeps the laptop warm by sleeping
on it and forces me to type one-handed whilst stroking her.

About the editor

Jane McMorland Hunter has compiled 13 poetry anthologies,
including collections on books, happiness, gardening, nature,
friendship, London, England and the First World War. She
also writes gardening, cookery, nature and craft books, has
been a gardener, potter and quilter and works at Hatchards
Bookshop in Piccadilly. She lives in London in a small house
overflowing with books.

Introduction

I would like to be able to say I grew up in a house where everyone cooked and I learnt my favourite recipes sitting at the kitchen table watching Mum, but I can't. She was actually a very good cook but could not see the point of it, and as soon as I went to school she announced that she was going to get a job and pay for us to eat out. Somehow she even managed to present the figures as if this would be an economy. We had an account at the local pub, the local chippy and a splendid sixties bistro where the tables were covered with red and white plastic cloths and the candles balanced in raffia-covered Chianti bottles. On the days when we didn't eat out we had 'ready meals', pies and frozen peas or roast dinners, which came in plastic trays. I loved it; I knew aeroplane food came on plastic trays and this seemed an exotic way of eating – it only gradually dawned on me that the various plastic dinners all tasted pretty much the same.

There were two cookery books at home: Marguerite Patten's *Cookery in Colour* and *Cooking with Elizabeth Craig*, the latter given to Mum by her grandmother in the forlorn hope that it would inspire a love of cooking. Neither was ever used and I regarded them with awe when I was learning to read as a child. *Cookery in Colour* did what it said on the cover, with enticing pictures of every recipe, and I devoured it in the same way that I read Enid Blyton's Famous Five series. At first I was seduced by the pictures but I soon discovered the wonderful worlds into which the words led me. Later I learned to cook. I still read recipe books as much, if not more, than I cook from them.

Eating is a necessity for all of us, but it is also bound up with the rituals of our lives. Everyday rituals such as breakfast, lunch and supper and rituals of celebration: weddings, birthdays, feasts and even fasts. This is not a comprehensive history of food writing,

7

nor is it a balanced collection of extracts. The pieces are taken from books I like, and I am obviously biased. So too are the writers; there is an abundance of writing on bread, breakfast and afternoon tea, while some foods and meals barely get a mention. I have included very few recipes (most of which I would not recommend trying) as I wanted to create a book which would appeal to the imagination as much as whetting the appetite.

Not all the writers included are chefs, or even particularly good cooks, but all (of necessity) are eaters and drinkers – most embarking on their meals with interest and sometimes even pleasure. Anticipation or remembrance of a meal is often as important as the meal itself, both for the glutton and for the starving. Travellers, explorers, vicars, diarists, poets and playwrights are all concerned with food, as are philosophers, lovers and novelists. The enthusiastic cook, the lazy eater, the rich and the poor all have their opinions and advice for the unwary cook, ranging from useful to useless. Pieces on drink are also here, including a sharp warning from G. K. Chesterton and an interesting recipe for mead from Sir Kenelm Digby.

Poets from Byron to Belloc, Herrick to Hardy and Langland to Lawrence have all written verse on food and feasts, inspired by, amongst other things, honeycombs, pots of tea and figs. In fiction, Louisa May Alcott and Charles Dickens describe the trials and tribulations of Christmas dinner, Tobias Smollett bemoans the horrors of haggis and Becky Sharp is caught unawares by chili. Elsewhere the Rev. James Woodforde tries swan and Jonathan Swift comes up with a shocking but modest proposal. Throughout history the rich suffer from over-eating, the poor and oppressed from hunger. We may be shocked at the over-indulgence of Romans such as Petronius, but culinary extravaganzas have continued down the centuries. Attitudes to food change and some readers may find some of the dishes recommended shocking or distasteful, but good, bad or even unacceptable foods provide excellent literary entertainment.

Compiling the longlist of potential pieces, I compiled an orderly survey, neatly divided by subject. One piece would highlight a particular aspect of food or dining, and I would wander off on a culinary and literary tangent. It made for interesting reading and unexpected finds so I have adopted the same technique for the ordering of extracts. You will find ice cream in summer and plum pudding in winter, and one or two entries follow on from each other, but most deliberately stand alone. Some people, I know, read these anthologies from start to finish, one piece per day, but I know also that many jump in and out as the fancy takes them. I would aim to be the first, but in reality I am very much the second, so I have arranged the pieces to suit both types of reader.

The pieces are taken from a variety of sources: recipe books, novels, prose, poetry, and fondly remembered stories from my childhood. Food and drink are often hidden in books, with the recipe for a perfect Martini to be found in a thriller and instructions on how to eat muffins in a play. There are some omissions due to space and copyright constraints, and the majority of pieces are taken from longer works, but in all cases I have given the original source. Some, such as Oliver asking for more or the contents of the Water Rat's picnic basket, will be well known to most readers, but my aim is that this collection will be a mix of favourites and surprises. I hope you enjoy it.

JANUARY

A Little Something

Timing

From *A Handbook of Cookery for a Small House, 1923*

Jessie Conrad (1873–1936)

Cooking ought not to take too much of one's time. One hour and a half to two hours for lunch, and two and a half for dinner is sufficient, providing that the servant knows how to make up the fire in order to get the stove ready for use. Most girls will quickly learn to do that and how to put a joint properly in the oven. For my part I never went into the kitchen before half-past eleven for a half-past one lunch of three dishes. But once the cooking is begun one must give all one's attention and care to it. No dish, however simple, will cook itself. You must not leave the kitchen while the cooking is going on – unless of necessity and only for a very few minutes at a time.

Ten Minutes

From *Cooking in Ten Minutes / La Cuisine en dix minutes, ou l'Adaptation au rythme moderne, 1930*

Édouard de Pomiane (1875–1964)

Translated by Peggie Benton

Preface:

I shall not try to explain or defend myself. I shall try to convince you by describing all the dishes that can be prepared in ten minutes, only, of course, in towns where the necessary materials can be obtained. If you have to catch your fish in a limpid stream before preparing it then you will need more than ten minutes, even if you devour it raw, sprinkled with salt.

My book is meant for the student, for the *midinette*, for the clerk, for the artist, for lazy people, poets, men of action, dreamers and scientists, for everyone who has only an hour for lunch or dinner and yet wants half an hour of peace to watch the smoke of a cigarette whilst they sip a cup of coffee which has not even time to get cold.

Modern life spoils so much that is pleasant. Let us see that it does not make us spoil our steak or our omelette. Ten minutes is sufficient – one minute more and all would be lost.

Cruella de Vil's Dinner Party

From *The Hundred and One Dalmatians, 1956*

Dodie Smith (1896–1990)

Cruella de Vil's dinner party took place in a room with black marble walls, on a white marble table. The food was rather unusual.

The soup was dark purple. And what did it taste of? Pepper!

The fish was bright green. And what did it taste of? Pepper!

The meat was pale blue. And what did that taste of? Pepper!

Everything tasted of pepper, even the ice-cream – which was black.

The Secret of Good Tea

From *In a German Pension: Germans at Meat, 1911*

Katherine Mansfield (1888–1923)

'Ah, that's one thing I *can* do,' said I, laughing brightly. 'I can make very good tea. The great secret is to warm the teapot.'

'Warm the teapot,' interrupted the Herr Rat, pushing away his soup plate. 'What do you warm the teapot for? Ha! ha! that's very good! One does not eat the teapot, I suppose?'

He fixed his cold blue eyes upon me with an expression which suggested a thousand premeditated invasions.

'So that is the great secret of your English tea? All you do is to warm the teapot.'

I wanted to say that was only the preliminary canter, but could not translate it, and so was silent.

First or Last?

From *The Constance Spry Cookery Book, 1956*

Constance Spry (1886–1960) and Rosemary Hume (1907–1984)

There is an argument concerning the serving of tea itself that might be aired here. China tea offered plain or with thin slices of lemon is pleasant to many of us, and the connoisseur will not accept it any other way, considering the addition of milk to so delicately flavoured a beverage as barbaric; even those who like to take it with milk insist that this shall be put in last. This brings us to the real argument. Leaving China tea out of the question, should tea be served with the milk poured in first or last? Those in favour of milk being put into the cup first will maintain, and rightly, I think, that the resulting cup of tea has a more blended taste. This is natural enough, because in pouring on to a small quantity of milk a larger quantity of scalding tea the milk becomes ever so slightly cooked. The difference in the taste of tea poured out in this way is less obvious in subsequent cups. Now those on the other side of the argument will say that in polite circles tea is poured first into the cups, and then they will add in good old-fashioned parlance 'and cream and sugar handed separately'; and it is when they use the word cream that they undermine their own argument. If you are serving tea with cream, the cream should not be put first into the cup because the scalding of it spoils its flavour. In old-fashioned tea parties cream was *de rigueur* with tea and should certainly have been put in last, but a little ordinary milk, or milk, shall we say, on the thin side, poured into a full cup of tea does not really appeal to a discerning taste. In the old days, when it was correct to hand the cream after the tea had been poured out, there was another custom. The hostess would rinse out the tea-cups with boiling water from her silver kettle before pouring in the tea. This was not with the sole object of warming the cups, but also to prevent her delicate china from becoming cracked by the sudden impact of hot tea. Now we are no longer all of us so meticulous in the matter of pouring out, the putting in of the milk first will have the same advantageous effect.

Cold Tea

From *Sons and Lovers, 1913* | D. H. Lawrence (1885–1930)

At a quarter to six he rose, cut two thick slices of bread and butter, and put them in the white calico snap-bag. He filled his tin bottle with tea. Cold tea without milk or sugar was the drink he preferred for the pit.

The Friendly Cinnamon Bun

Russell Hoban (1925–2011)

Shining in his stickiness and glistening with honey,
safe among his sisters and his brothers on a tray,
with raisin eyes that looked at me as I put down my money,
there smiled a friendly cinnamon bun, and this I heard him say:

'It's a lovely, lovely morning, and the world's a lovely place;
I know it's going to be a lovely day.
I know we're going to be good friends; I like your honest face;
Together we might go a long, long way.'

The baker's girl rang up the sale, 'I'll wrap your bun,' said she.
'Oh no, you needn't bother,' I replied.
I smiled back at that cinnamon bun and ate him, one two three,
and walked out with his friendliness inside.

Minding What You Eat

From *The Life of Samuel Johnson, 1791* | James Boswell (1740–1795)

Samuel Johnson (1709–1784)

Samuel Johnson:

Some people have a foolish way of not minding, or pretending not to mind, what they eat. For my part, I mind my belly very studiously, and very carefully; for I look upon it, that he who does not mind his belly will hardly mind anything else.

8 January

Late for Breakfast

From *Jack Abbott's Breakfast, 1847* | Leigh Hunt (1784–1859)

'What a breakfast I shall eat!' thought Jack Abbott, as he turned into Middle Temple Lane, towards the chambers of his old friend and tutor Goodall. 'How I shall swill the tea! how cram down the rolls (especially the inside bits)! how apologize for "one cup more !" – But Goodall is an excellent old fellow – he won't mind. To be sure I'm rather late. The rolls, I'm afraid, will be cold, or double baked; but anything will be delicious. If I met a baker, I could eat his basket.'

. . . .

Unfortunately for the hero of our story, this angel of sixty-five, unshaved, and with stockings down at heel, had a memory which could not recollect what had been told him six hours before, much less six days. Accordingly, he had finished his breakfast, and given his cat the remaining drop of milk long before his (in every sense of the word) late pupil presented himself within his threshold.

Wine Lists

From *The Chronicles of Clovis: The Chaplet, 1911*

Saki / H. H. Munro (1870–1916)

The earlier stages of the dinner had worn off. The wine lists had been consulted, by some with the blank embarrassment of a schoolboy suddenly called on to locate a Minor Prophet in the tangled hinterland of the Old Testament, by others with the severe scrutiny which suggests that they have visited most of the higher-priced wines in their own homes and probed their family weaknesses. The diners who chose their wine in the latter fashion always gave their orders in a penetrating voice, with a plentiful garnishing of stage directions. By insisting on having your bottle pointing to the north when the cork is being drawn, and calling the waiter Max, you may induce an impression on your guests which hours of laboured boasting might be powerless to achieve. For this purpose, however, the guests must be chosen as carefully as the wine.

Thick Milk for Breakfast

From *Plain Cookery for the Working Classes, 1852*

Charles Elmé Francatelli (1805–1876)

Milk, buttermilk, or even skim-milk, will serve for this purpose. To every pint of milk, mix a piled-up table-spoonful of flour, and stir the mixture while boiling on the fire for ten minutes; season with a little salt, and eat it with bread or a boiled potato. This kind of food is well adapted for the breakfast of women and children, and is far preferable to a sloppy mess of tea, which comes to more money.

Spoons

From *Travels and Researches in South Africa, 1857*

David Livingstone (1813–1873)

They [the villagers] bring forth also large pots and bowls of thick milk; some contain six or eight gallons; and each of these, as well as of the beer, is given to a particular person, who has the power to divide it with whom he pleases. The head man of any section of the tribe is generally selected for this office. Spoons not being generally in fashion, the milk is conveyed to the mouth with the hand. I often presented my friends with iron spoons, and it was curious to observe how their habit of hand-eating prevailed, though they were delighted with the spoons. They lifted out a little with the utensil, then put it on the left hand, and ate it out of that.

12 January

Dining with the Houyhnhnms

From *Gulliver's Travels: A Voyage to the Houyhnhnms, 1726*

Jonathan Swift (1667–1745)

When Dinner was done, the Master Horse took me aside, and by
Signs and Words made me understand the concern he was in that
I had nothing to eat. Oats in their Tongue are called *Hlunnh*. This
Word I pronounced two or three times; for although I had refused
them at first, yet, upon second Thoughts, I considered that I could
contrive to make of them a Kind of Bread, which might be sufficient,
with Milk, to keep me alive, till I could make my Escape to some
other Country, and to Creatures of my own Species. The Horse
immediately ordered a white Mare-servant of his Family to bring me
a good Quantity of Oats in a Sort of wooden Tray. These I heated
before the Fire, as well as I could, and rubbed them till the Husks
came off, which I made a shift to winnow from the Grain; I ground
and beat them between two Stones, then took Water, and made them
into a Paste or Cake, which I toasted at the Fire and eat warm with
Milk. It was at first a very insipid Diet, though common enough
in many Parts of Europe, but grew tolerable by Time; and having
been often reduced to hard Fare in my Life, this was not the first
Experiment I had made how easily Nature is satisfied. And I
cannot but observe, that I never had one Hour's Sickness while
I staied in this island.

Colourings to Stain Jellies, Ices or Cakes

From *A New System of Domestic Cookery, 1806, 1816*

A Lady / Mrs Rundell (1745–1828)

For a beautiful *red*, boil fifteen grains of cochineal in the finest powder, with a dram and a half of cream of tartar, in half a pint of water, very slowly, half an hour. Add in boiling a bit of alum the size of a pea. Or use beet-root sliced, and some liquor poured over.

For *white*, use almonds finely powdered, with a little drop of water; or use cream.

For *yellow*, yolks of eggs, or a bit of saffron steeped in the liquor and squeezed.

For *green*, pound spinach-leaves or beet-leaves, express the juice, and boil in a tea-cupful in a saucepan of water to take off the rawness.

For the Several Colours of Tarts

From *The Accomplisht Cook, 1660* | Robert May (1588–c.1664)

If to have them yellow, preserved quinces, apricocks, necturnes, and melacattons, boil them up in white-wine with sugar, and strain them. Otherways, strained yolks of eggs and cream.

For green tarts take green quodlings, green preserved apricocks, green preserved plums, green grapes, and green gooseberries.

For red tarts, quinces, pippins, cherries, rasberries, barberries, red currans, red gooseberries, damsins.

For black tarts, prunes, and many other berries preserved.

For white tarts, whites of eggs and cream.

Of all manner of tart-stuff strained, that carries his colour black, as prunes, damsons, &c. For lard of set Tarts dishes, or patty-pans.

The Problems

From *Cooking in a Bedsitter, 1961, 1963*

Katharine Whitehorn (1928–2021)

Cooking a decent meal in a bedsitter is not just a matter of finding something that can be cooked over a single gas-ring. It is a problem of finding somewhere to put down the fork while you take the lid off the saucepan, and then finding somewhere else to put the lid. It is finding a place to keep the butter where it will not get mixed up with your razor or your hairpins. It is having your hands covered with flour, and a pot boiling over onto your landlady's carpet, and no water to mop up any of it nearer than the bathroom at the other end of the landing. It is cooking at floor level, in a hurry, with nowhere to put the salad but the washing-up bowl, which in any case is full of socks.

However, with imagination, common sense, and a great deal of newspaper, all this can be surmounted; and an excellent meal can be cooked without fuss even in the daintiest of lodgings.

Bedouin Feast

From *The Seven Pillars of Wisdom, 1926* | T. E. Lawrence (1888–1935)

The first dip, for me, at least, was always cautious, since the liquid fat was so hot that my unaccustomed fingers could seldom bear it: and so I would toy with an exposed and cooling lump of meat till others' excavations had drained my rice-segment. We would knead between the fingers (not soiling the palm), neat balls of rice and fat and liver and meat cemented by gentle pressure, and project them by leverage of the thumb from the crooked fore-finger into the mouth. With the right trick and the right construction the little lump held together and came clean off the hand; but when surplus butter and odd fragments clung, cooling, to the fingers, they had to be licked carefully to make the next effort slip easier away.

As the meat pile wore down (nobody really cared about rice: flesh was the luxury) one of the chief Howeitat eating with us would draw his dagger, silver hilted, set with turquoise, a signed masterpiece of Mohammed ibn Zari, of Jauf, and would cut criss-cross from the larger bones long diamonds of meat easily torn up between the fingers; for it was necessarily boiled very tender, since all had to be disposed of with the right hand which alone was honourable.

Our host stood by the circle, encouraging the appetite with pious ejaculations. At top speed we twisted, tore, cut and stuffed: never speaking, since conversation would insult a meal's quality; though it was proper to smile thanks when an intimate guest passed a select fragment, or when Mohammed el Dheilan gravely handed over a huge barren bone with a blessing. On such occasions I would return the compliment with some hideous impossible lump of guts, a flippancy which rejoiced the Howeitat, but which the gracious, aristocratic Nasir saw with disapproval.

Marmalade

From *Perfume from Provence, 1935* | Winifred Fortescue (1888–1951)

When the harvest of orange-blossom is plucked and the wild oranges turn golden, everyone picks them for *confiture d'oranges*, a delicious bitter marmalade.

Neighbours this year vied with each other in showering these wild oranges upon us until Emilia, grown desperate, announced her intention of making marmalade at once. From that moment everything in the house became sticky. Emilia and Lucienne were up to the eyes in marmalade. The kitchen table and all that was laid thereon became coated with it. Forks, spoons, and knives stuck to our hands; plates clung to the tablecloth. The smell of cooking oranges pervaded the whole house; every casserole and kitchen vessel was filled with soaking oranges; the stove completely covered with preserving pans, some of them borrowed from an obliging American neighbour. Even our *lingerie* was stiffened with marmalade after the sticky hands of Lucienne had ironed and folded it; for in Provence the maids do all the household ironing as part of their job.

When a mass of pots were filled and I had soaked papers in brandy to preserve the marmalade, and we had tied on the covers and labelled the jars, Emilia proudly invited *Monsieur* to enter her 'jam-shop.' When he made his enthusiastic exit, his feet stuck to the parquet in his study. He had been paddling in marmalade.

The Lemon-house

From *Twilight in Italy, 1916* | D. H. Lawrence (1885–1930)

Between the lemon trees, beside the path, were little orange trees, and dozens of oranges hanging like hot coals in the twilight. When I warm my hands at them the Signore breaks me off one twig after another, till I have a bunch of burning oranges among dark leaves, a heavy bouquet. Looking down the Hades of the lemon-house, the many ruddy-clustered oranges beside the path remind me of the lights of a village along the lake at night, while the pale lemons above are the stars. There is a subtle, exquisite scent of lemon flowers. Then I notice a citron. He hangs heavy and bloated upon so small a tree, that he seems a dark green enormity. There is a great host of lemons overhead, half-visible, a swarm of ruddy oranges by the paths, and here and there a fat citron. It is almost like being under the sea.

By the Bed-side

From *The Eve of St Agnes* | John Keats (1795–1821)

XXIX

    Then by the bed-side, where the faded moon
    Made a dim, silver twilight, soft he set
    A table, and, half anguish'd, threw thereon
    A cloth of woven crimson, gold, and jet:–
    O for some drowsy Morphean amulet!
    The boisterous, midnight, festive clarion,
    The kettle-drum, and far-heard clarinet,
    Affray his ears, though but in dying tone:–
The hall door shuts again, and all the noise is gone.

XXX

    And still she slept an azure-lidded sleep,
    In blanched linen, smooth, and lavender'd,
    While he forth from the closet brought a heap
    Of candied apple, quince, and plum, and gourd;
    With jellies soother than the creamy curd,
    And lucent syrops, tinct with cinnamon;
    Manna and dates, in argosy transferr'd
    From Fez; and spiced dainties, every one,
From silken Samarcand to cedar'd Lebanon.

XXXI

    These delicates he heap'd with glowing hand
    On golden dishes and in baskets bright
    Of wreathed silver: sumptuous they stand
    In the retired quiet of the night,
    Filling the chilly room with perfume light.–
    'And now, my love, my seraph fair, awake!
    Thou art my heaven, and I thine eremite:
    Open thine eyes, for meek St. Agnes' sake,
Or I shall drowse beside thee, so my soul doth ache.'

How Not to Boil an Egg

From *How to Cook a Wolf,* *1942* | M. F. K. Fisher (1908–1992)

The simplest way to eat an egg, if you refuse to swallow it raw, even in its fanciest high-tasting disguises, is to boil it. Rather it is *not* to boil it, for no more erroneous phrase ever existed than 'to boil an egg'.

There are several ways *not* to boil an egg so that it will be tender, thoroughly cooked, and yet almost as easily digested as if it were raw.

One fairly good way is to drop the egg gently into simmering water, first running cold water over it so that it will not crack, and then let it stand there in the gentle heat for whatever time you wish. It will cook just as fast as if the water was hopping about in great bubbles, and it will be a better-treated egg, once opened.

Another way, which I think is the best one, is to cover the egg with cold water in a little pan. Heat it briskly, and as soon as it begins to bubble, the egg is done. It will be tenderer than when started in hot water, which of course makes the part nearest the shell cook immediately, instead of heating the whole thing gently.

To Boil Eggs

From *The Closet of the Eminently Learned Sir Kenelme Digbie Kt. Opened, 1669* | Sir Kenelm Digby (1603–1665)

A certain and infallible method to boil new-laid Eggs to sup up, and yet that they have the white turned to milk, is thus: Break a very little hole, at the bigger end of the shell, and put it into the water, whiles it boileth. Let it remain boiling, whiles your Pulse beateth two hundred stroaks. Then take it out immediately, and you will find it of an exact temper: others put Eggs into boyling water just as you take it from the fire, and let them remain there, till the water be so cooled, that you may just put in your hand, and take out the Eggs.

Others put the Eggs into cold water, which they set upon the fire, and as soon as the water begins to boil, the Eggs are enough.

A Catch

Dean Henry Aldrich (1647–1710)

If all be true that I do think,
There are five reasons we should drink:
Good wine; a friend; or being dry;
Or lest we should be, by and by;
Or any other reason why.

A Little Something

From *Winnie-the-Pooh, 1926* | A. A. Milne (1882–1956)

Pooh always liked a little something at eleven o'clock in the morning, and he was very glad to see Rabbit getting out the plates and mugs; and when Rabbit said, 'Honey or condensed milk with your bread?' he was so excited that he said, 'Both,' and then, so as not to seem greedy, he added, 'But don't bother about the bread, please.' And for a long time after that he said nothing … until at last, humming to himself in a rather sticky voice, he got up, shook Rabbit lovingly by the paw, and said that he must be going on.

'Must you?' said Rabbit politely.

'Well,' said Pooh, 'I could stay a little longer if it – if you –' and he tried very hard to look in the direction of the larder.

'As a matter of fact,' said Rabbit, 'I was going out myself directly.'

'Oh well, then, I'll be going on. Good-bye.'

'Well, good-bye, if you're sure you won't have any more.'

'*Is* there any more?' asked Pooh quickly.

Rabbit took the covers off the dishes, and said, 'No, there wasn't.'

'I thought not,' said Pooh, nodding to himself. 'Well. Good-bye. I must be going on.'

To a Haggis

Robert Burns (1759–1796)

Fair fa' your honest, sonsie face,
Great chieftain o' the puddin-race!
Aboon them a' ye tak your place,
   Painch, tripe, or thairm:
Weel are ye wordy o' a grace
   As lang 's my arm.

The groaning trencher there ye fill,
Your hurdies like a distant hill,
Your pin wad help to mend a mill
   In time o' need;
While thro' your pores the dews distil
   Like amber bead.

His knife see rustic Labour dight,
An' cut ye up wi' ready sleight,
Trenching your gushing entrails bright,
   Like ony ditch;
And then, O what a glorious sight,
   Warm-reekin, rich!

Then, horn for horn, they stretch an' strive:
Deil tak the hindmost! on they drive,
Till a' their weel-swall'd kytes belyve
   Are bent like drums;
Then auld guidman, maist like to rive,
   Bethankit hums.

Is there that o'er his French ragout,
Or olio that wad staw a sow,
Or fricassee wad mak her spew
    Wi' perfect sconner,
Looks down wi' sneering, scornfu' view
    On sic a dinner?

Poor devil! see him owre his trash,
As feckless as a wither'd rash,
His spindle shank a guid whip-lash,
    His nieve a nit;
Thro' bloody flood or field to dash,
    O how unfit!

But mark the Rustic, haggis-fed –
The trembling earth resounds his tread!
Clap in his walie nieve a blade,
    He'll make it whissle;
An' legs, an' arms, an' heads will sned,
    Like taps o' thrissle.

Ye Pow'rs wha mak mankind your care,
And dish them out their bill o' fare,
Auld Scotland wants nae skinking ware
    That jaups in luggies;
But, if ye wish her gratefu' prayer,
    Gie her a Haggis!

Covering Up

From *Directions to Servants: Directions to the Footman, published posthumously, 1745* | Jonathan Swift (1667–1745)

If you are bringing up a Joint of Meat in a Dish, and it falls out of your Hand, before you get into the Dining Room, with the Meat on the Ground, and the Sauce spilled, take up the Meat gently, wipe it with the Lap of your Coat, then put it again into the Dish, and serve it up; and when your Lady misses the Sauce, tell her, it is to be sent up in a Plate by itself.

Too Hot to Eat

From *Bone in the Throat*, 1995 (USA), 2000 (UK)

Anthony Bourdain (1956–)

Two-hundred-and-eighty-pound Salvatore Pitera, in a powder-blue jogging suit and tinted aviator glasses, stepped out of Frank's Original Pizza onto Spring Street. He had a slice of pizza in one hand, too hot to eat, and he was blowing on it as he waddled through street traffic.

At the corner of Elizabeth Street, he passed the social club. A group of old men sat out front, in tattered easy chairs, drinking espresso.

'Hey, Wig! Sally Wig!' one of the men called out to him. The old men laughed. One man, the oldest, in a dark jacket and unbuttoned white dress shirt, put down his demitasse. 'Hey Sally, what you walking so funny for? You got the piles or something?'

'I don't want to get any fuckin' pizza on my shoes.' Sally said.

'Hey, Wig,' said another espresso drinker. 'Looking good.'

The old men laughed. Sally kept walking west, his face all red now, jaw clenched, both eyes on his new Bally running shoes. When he was out of sight of the old men, he reached up to feel if his hair was on right.

A Winter Picnic

From *Elizabeth and Her German Garden, 1898*

Elizabeth von Arnim (1866–1941)

January 28th

Yesterday, by way of a change, we went for a picnic to the shores
of the Baltic, ice-bound at this season, and utterly desolate at our
nearest point. I have a weakness for picnics, especially in winter.

. . . .

I warmed soup in a little apparatus I have for such occasions,
which helped to take the chilliness off the sandwiches, – this is the
only unpleasant part of a winter picnic, the clammy quality of the
provisions just when you most long for something very hot.

Advice

From *The Art of Cookery, In Imitation of Horace's Art of Poetry, 1708* | William King (1663–1712)

Crowd not your table; let your numbers be
Not more than sev'n, and never less than three.
'Tis the dessert that graces all the feast,
For an ill end disparages the rest;
A thousand things well done, and one forgot
Defaces obligation by that blot.
Make your transparent sweetmeats truly nice,
With Indian sugar and Arabian spice;
And let your various creams encircled be
With swelling fruit just ravish'd from the tree.
Let plates and dishes be from China brought,
With lively paint and earth transparent wrought.
The feast now done, discourses are renew'd,
And witty arguments with mirth pursu'd.
The cheerful master midst his jovial friends
His glass 'To their best wishes' recommends.
The grace-cup follows 'To his sov'reign's health,'
And to his country 'Plenty, peace and wealth.'
Performing then the piety of grace
Each man that pleases reassumes his place;
While at his gate from such abundant store,
He show'rs his godlike blessings on the poor.

A Splendid Banquet

From *The Satires: Book II, Satire VIII, c. 30 BC* |

Horace / Quintus Horatius Flaccus (65–8 BC)

Translated by Rev. Francis Howes (1776–1844)

Dialogue between Horace and Fundanius:

I hope you liked the banquet, which they say
The splendid Rufus gave you yesterday.
For, when I wish'd you to partake my fare,
I found you had been long carousing there.
'Troth, never merrier in my life before.
'What first came on? 'A huge Lucanian boar,
Caught, as we heard the master oft declare,
What time the southern breeze blew fresh and fair.
Rapes, lettuce, radishes were round it placed,
With sundry sauces pungent to the taste.
And form'd the jaded appetite to teaze.
As skirwort, pickled shad, and Coan lees.

   This course withdrawn, a purple rug restored
Its brilliant beauty to the maple board;
Another slave swept up the scraps that fell,
That nothing might offend the sight or smell.
Advancing next with step demure and staid,
Slow as at Ceres' rites the Attic maid,
The swart Hydaspes bore Caecubian wine, –
Alcon pure Chian undebased with brine.

   Then thus our host bespoke his noble guest
'Are these the wines, my Lord, you relish best?
'If those of Alban or Falernian growth
'Please more, pray speak the word – we have them both'.

Kippers

From *A Handbook of Cookery for a Small House, 1923*

Jessie Conrad (1873–1936)

Kippers are difficult to cook without smell and to keep moist.
The best way is to lay the kipper on its back in a flat meat dish.
A small piece of butter should be always put into the dish first and
a larger piece on the open side of the kipper, with a little white paper.
Put into a quick oven for fifteen to twenty minutes. There
will be no smell.

31 January

FEBRUARY

A Baker's Bow-window

The Railway Buffet

From *A Bear Called Paddington, 1958* | Michael Bond (1926–2017)

'Well, Paddington,' said Mr Brown, as he placed two steaming cups of tea on the table and a plate piled high with cakes. 'How's that to be going on with?'

Paddington's eyes glistened. 'It's very nice, thank you,' he exclaimed, eyeing the tea doubtfully. 'But it's rather hard drinking out of a cup. I usually get my head stuck, or else my hat falls in and makes it taste nasty.'

Mr Brown hesitated. 'Then you'd better give your hat to me. I'll pour the tea into a saucer for you. It's not really done in the best circles, but I'm sure no one will mind just this once.'

Paddington removed his hat and laid it carefully on the table while Mr Brown poured out the tea. He looked hungrily at the cakes, in particular at a large cream-and-jam one which Mr Brown placed on the plate in front of him.

'There you are, Paddington,' he said. 'I'm sorry they haven't any marmalade ones, but they were the best I could get.'

'I'm glad I emigrated,' said Paddington, as he reached out a paw and pulled the plate nearer. 'Do you think anyone would mind if I stood on the table to eat?'

Before Mr Brown could answer he had climbed up and placed his paw firmly on the bun. It was a very large bun, the biggest and stickiest Mr Brown had been able to find, and in a matter of moments most of the inside found its way on to Paddington's whiskers. People started to nudge each other and began staring in their direction. Mr Brown wished he had chosen a plain, ordinary bun, but he wasn't very experienced in the ways of bears. He stirred his tea and looked out of the window, pretending he had tea with a bear on Paddington station every day of his life.

Discovering France

From *Chez Panisse Fruit, 2002* | Alice Waters (1944–)

I did not begin to pay attention to food in earnest until I was nineteen years old. I was luckier than most American children who grew up in the 1950s in that I was exposed to at least some foods that were pure, un-processed, fresh and seasonal. My parents planted a vegetable garden in our New Jersey back yard where they grew corn, beans, and tomatoes; my sisters and I foraged for wild blueberries in New Hampshire in July; and our suburban town had not yet spilled out of its borders and buried the small orchards and truck farms that surrounded it.

But nothing prepared me for the food of France, where I went for my junior year of college. There, for the first time in my life, I learned that good food could be a serious pleasure and that its pursuit was worthy of the utmost concentration and discrimination. In France people not only gave deep thought to their next meal; they surrendered themselves utterly to its sensual enjoyment.

It was a year of a thousand epiphanies: the bread fresh from the wood-burning oven of my neighborhood bakery; the cheese so unimaginably and ripely various; the staggering bounty of the sea, still glistening and alive at the fishmonger's; the long meals with my new French friends, whose passion for food was so grown-up in its refinement and so childlike in its exuberance.

On Food

Hilaire Belloc (1870–1953)

Alas! What various tastes in food
Divide the human brotherhood!
Birds in their little nests agree
With Chinamen, but not with me.
Colonials like their oysters hot,
Their omelettes heavy – I do not.
The French are fond of slugs and frogs,
The Siamese eat puppy dogs.
The nobles at the brilliant court
Of Muscovy consumed a sort
Of candles held and eaten thus,
As though they were asparagus.
The Spaniard, I have heard it said,
Eats garlic, by itself on bread:
Now just suppose a friend or dun
Dropped in to lunch at half-past one
And you were jovially to say,
'Here's bread and garlic! Peg away!'
I doubt if you would gain your end
Or soothe the dun, or please the friend.
In Italy the traveller notes
With great disgust the flesh of goats
Appearing on the table d'hôtes;
And even this the natives spoil
By frying it in rancid oil.
In Maryland they charge like sin
For nasty stuff called terrapin;
And when they ask you out to dine

At Washington, instead of wine,
They give you water from the spring
With lumps of ice for flavouring,
That sometimes kill and always freeze
The high plenipotentiaries.
In Massachusetts all the way
From Boston down to Buzzards Bay
They feed you till you want to die
On rhubarb pie and pumpkin pie,
And horrible huckleberry pie,
And when you summon strength to cry,
'What is there else that I can try?'
They stare at you in mild surprise
And serve you other kinds of pies.
And I with these mine eyes have seen
A dreadful stuff called Margarine
Consumed by men in Bethnal Green.
But I myself that here complain
Confess restriction quite in vain.
I feel my native courage fail
To see a Gascon eat a snail;
I dare not ask abroad for tea;
No cannibal can dine with me;
And all the world is torn and rent
By varying views on nutriment.
And yet upon the other hand,
De gustibus non disputand –

– Um

A Table Centrepiece

From *The Diary of a Country Parson, 1783*

James Woodforde (1740–1803)

Dinner with the Bishop, 4 September:
A most beautiful Artificial Garden in the Centre of the Table
remained at Dinner and afterwards, it was one of the prettiest
things I ever saw, about a Yard long, and about 18 Inches wide, in
the middle of which was a high round Temple supported on round
Pillars, the Pillars were wreathed round with artificial Flowers –
on one side was a Shepherdess on the other a Shepherd, several
handsome Urns decorated with artificial Flowers also &c. &c.

The Table

From *To the Lighthouse, 1927* | Virginia Woolf (1882–1941)

Now eight candles were stood down the table, and after the first
stoop the flames stood upright and drew with them into visibility
the long table entire, and in the middle a yellow and purple dish of
fruit. What had she done with it, Mrs. Ramsay wondered, for Rose's
arrangement of the grapes and pears, of the horny pink-lined shell,
of the bananas, made her think of a trophy fetched from the bottom
of the sea, of Neptune's banquet, of the bunch that hangs with vine
leaves over the shoulder of Bacchus (in some picture), among the
leopard skins and the torches lolloping red and gold ... Thus brought
up suddenly into the light it seemed possessed of great size and
depth, was like a world in which one could take one's staff and climb
hills, she thought, and go down into valleys, and to her pleasure (for
it brought them into sympathy momentarily) she saw that Augustus
too feasted his eyes on the same plate of fruit, plunged in, broke
off a bloom there, a tassel here, and returned, after feasting, to his
hive. That was his way of looking, different from hers. But looking
together united them.

Now all the candles were lit up, and the faces on both sides of
the table were brought nearer by the candle light, and composed, as
they had not been in the twilight, into a party round a table, for the
night was now shut off by panes of glass, which, far from giving any
accurate view of the outside world, rippled it so strangely that here,
inside the room, seemed to be order and dry land; there, outside, a
reflection in which things waved and vanished, waterily.

The Dining Room

From *Pantropheon, 1853* | Alexis Soyer (1810–1858)

The *cœnaculum* (dining-room), properly so called, was the place in the upper part of the house where they eat. It was reached by a staircase, and thither persons repaired during the summer, particularly in the country. The Roman villas terminated by a platform, on which the Romans often collected at meal-time; the air was not so hot, and the panorama of the neighbouring country-seats was presented without obstruction, to the gaze of the guests.

The dining-room was commonly decorated with fasces of arms and trophies, which served as a momento of the warlike virtues of the ancestors of the master of the house. Enchanting frescoes stood out marvellously from the obscure shading of the wall, round which were twined fresh garlands of flowers; and a mosaic floor – master-piece of art and patience – harmonised with the fascinating landscape of the ceiling, the site of which varied with every course.

The Emperor Nero, who carried this taste for the beautiful rather too far, devised a sort of vault, in the most elegant style, and entirely composed of movable leaves of ivory, which exhaled sweet perfumes, and whence flowers fell on the guests. In another of his dining-rooms admiration was excited by a magnificent dome, the rotary movement of which imitated, day and night, the course of the celestial bodies. These prodigies of ancient mechanism adorned the palace that the prodigal Cæsar called 'the gilded house.' The colossal statue of that prince rose in the middle of the hall: it was 120 feet high!

Studious people, or those who wished to appear so, covered some part of the dining-room with books; for it was a custom introduced into Rome to have recitations or readings during the repast. Atticus had always a reader; and Juvenal promises the friend he invites to supper that he shall hear some fragments from Virgil and Homer.

The Greeks yielded willingly to this intellectual pastime at the commencement of the banquet, whilst incense and other perfumes filled the room with a light vapour.

Posh

From *Mortal Engines, 2001* | Philip Reeve (1966–)

Tom and Hester are aboard the pirate suburb Tunbridge Wheels. The mayor, His Worship Chrysler Peavey, realises Tom is a 'High London gent' and gives them a guided tour of the Town Hall:

Then it was time for afternoon tea in his private quarters, a room full of looted treasures high in the Town Hall where his rabble of whining, snot-nosed children kept getting under everybody's feet. His eldest daughter Cortina brought tea in delicate porcelain cups, and cucumber sandwiches on a blast-glass tray. She was a dim, terrified girl with watery blue eyes, and when her father saw that she hadn't cut the crusts off the sandwiches he knocked her backwards over the pouffe. 'Thomas 'ere is from LONDON!' he shouted, hurling the sandwiches at her. 'He expects fings POSH! And you should have done 'em in little TRIANGLES!'

Fashionable Tea

From *The Importance of Being Earnest, 1895*

Oscar Wilde (1854–1900)

CECILY: May I offer you some tea, Miss Fairfax?

GWENDOLEN: *(With elaborate politeness)* Thank you. *(Aside)* Detestable girl! But I require tea!

CECILY: *(Sweetly)* Sugar?

GWENDOLEN: *(Superciliously)* No, thank you. Sugar is not fashionable any more.

Cecily *looks angrily at her, takes up the tongs and puts four lumps of sugar into the cup*

CECILY: *(Severely)* Cake or bread and butter?

GWENDOLEN: *(In a bored manner)* Bread and butter, please. Cake is rarely seen at the best houses nowadays.

CECILY: *(Cuts a very large slice of cake, and puts it on the tray)* Hand that to Miss Fairfax.

Merriman *does so, and goes out with* footman. Gwendolen *drinks the tea and makes a grimace. Puts down cup at once, reaches out her hand to the bread and butter, looks at it, and finds it is cake. Rises in indignation*

GWENDOLEN: You have filled my tea with lumps of sugar, and though I asked most distinctly for bread and butter, you have given me cake. I am known for the gentleness of my disposition, and the extraordinary sweetness of my nature, but I warn you, Miss Cardew, you may go too far.

The Song of Right and Wrong

G. K. Chesterton (1874–1936)

Feast on wine or fast on water
And your honour shall stand sure,
God Almighty's son and daughter
He the valiant, she the pure;
If an angel out of heaven
Brings you other things to drink,
Thank him for his kind attentions,
Go and pour them down the sink.

Tea is like the East he grows in,
A great yellow Mandarin
With urbanity of manner
And unconsciousness of sin;
All the women, like a harem,
At his pig-tail troop along;
And, like all the East he grows in,
He is Poison when he's strong.

Tea, although an Oriental,
Is a gentleman at least;
Cocoa is a cad and coward,
Cocoa is a vulgar beast,
Cocoa is a dull, disloyal,
Lying, crawling cad and clown,
And may very well be grateful
To the fool that takes him down.

As for all the windy waters,
They were rained like tempests down
When good drink had been dishonoured
By the tipplers of the town;
When red wine had brought red ruin
And the death-dance of our times,
Heaven sent us Soda Water
As a torment for our crimes.

To Make Coffee

From *The Cooks and Confectioners Dictionary, 1723*

John Nott (late 17th–early 18th century)

To make Coffee

Take running, or River-Water, boil it, and put to a Quart, either one, two, or three Ounces of Coffee, as you like it, and let it boil only so long, as 'till the Coffee falls down.

Another better Way

Take running, or River-Water, put your Coffee in cold; mix it well with the Water, set them over the Fire, and let them warm, heat and scald, and boil them together, 'till the Coffee sinks; then take it off, let it settle and drink it.

Another the best Way

When you have drank off a Pot of Coffee, put into the Pot to the Grounds, as much Water, as you design to make the next time, and boil them together; then take the Pot off the Fire, and let it stand to settle a quarter of an Hour; then pour off the clear Liquor, cast away the Grounds, wash the Coffee-Pot; then put in the Coffee you would make next time, pour the Liquor in scalding hot, and let them stand to infuse, 'till you use it; then set it on the Fire, let them warm and heat leisurely, 'till it boils, 'till all the Coffee is well boil'd down, then let it settle and drink it.

Shrove Tuesday

From *Chocolat, 1999* | Joanne Harris (1964–)

The first night in the village:
We have gas but as yet no electricity. On our first night I made
pancakes for Anouk by candlelight and we ate them by the fireside,
using an old magazine for plates, as none of our things can be
delivered until tomorrow. The shop was originally a bakery and still
carries the baker's wheatsheaf carved above the narrow doorway, but
the floor is thick with a floury dust.

Nautical Pies

From *The Far Side of the World, 1984* | Patrick O'Brian (1914–2000)

'Pies at sea,' he [Jack] said, 'are made on nautical lines, of course. They are quite unlike pies by land. First you lay down a stratum of pastry, then a layer of meat, then a layer of pastry, then another layer of meat, and so on, according to the number of decks required. This is a three-decker, as you can see: spar-deck, main-deck, middle-deck, lower-deck.'

'But that makes four decks, my dear sir,' said Martin.

'Oh yes,' said Jack. 'All first-rate ships of the line, all three-deckers have four. And by counting the orlop you could make it five; or even six, with the poop. We only call them three-deckers, you understand. Though now I come to think of it, perhaps when we say deck we really mean the space between two of them.'

Promises and Pie-crusts

From *A Complete Collection of Genteel and Ingenious Conversation, Dialogue 1, 1738* | Jonathan Swift (1667–1745)

Lady Answerable: Promises and Pie-crust are made to be broken.

Loving Cup

From *Venus in the Kitchen: or Love's Cookery Book, 1952*

Norman Douglas (1868–1952)

Put in a bowl some toasted bread; add six ounces of sugar, one lump of sugar saturated in orange-flower essence; grate half a nutmeg and mix it with the same quantity of cinnamon and ginger in powder. Put this in a bowl together with a quart of good ale, one bottle of sherry, and a little soda-water.

The soda-water is the least important of these ingredients, and can be dispensed with.

La Celeste Praline: Chocolaterie Artisanale

From *Chocolat, 1999* | Joanne Harris (1964–)

15th February, the display window:

On a white marble shelf are aligned innumerable boxes, packages, *cornets* of silver and gold paper, rosettes, bells, flowers, hearts and long curls of multicoloured ribbon. In glass bells and dishes lie the chocolates, the pralines, Venus's nipples, truffles, *mendicants*, candied fruits, hazelnut clusters, chocolate seashells, candied rose-petals, sugared violets ... Protected from the sun by the half-blind which shields them, they gleam darkly, like sunken treasure, Aladdin's cave of sweet clichés. And in the middle she has built a magnificent centrepiece. A gingerbread house, walls of chocolate-coated *pain d'épices* with the detail piped on in silver and gold icing, roof tiles of florentines, studded with crystallized fruits, strange vines of icing and chocolate growing up the walls, marzipan birds singing in chocolate trees ... And the witch herself, dark chocolate from the top of her pointed hat to the hem of her long cloak half-astride a broomstick which is in reality a giant *guimauve*, the long twisted marshmallows that dangle from the stalls of sweet-vendors on carnival days.

15 February

Cookery in England

From *To the Lighthouse, 1927* | Virginia Woolf (1882–1941)

What passes for cookery in England is an abomination (they agreed). It is putting cabbages in water. It is roasting meat till it is like leather. It is cutting off the delicious skins of vegetables. 'In which,' said Mr. Bankes, 'all the virtue of the vegetable is contained.' And the waste, said Mrs. Ramsay. A whole French family could live on what an English cook throws away.

A Winter Fire-side

From *Confessions of an English Opium Eater, 1821*

Thomas De Quincey (1785–1859)

I put up a petition annually, for as much snow, hail, frost, or storm,
of one kind or other, as the skies can possibly afford us. Surely every
body is aware of the divine pleasures which attend a winter fire-side:
candles at four o'clock, warm hearth rugs, tea, a fair tea-maker,
shutters closed, curtains flowing in ample draperies on the floor,
whilst the wind and rain are raging audibly without.

Air

From *The Grub-Street Opera, Act III, Scene II, 1731*

Henry Fielding (1707–1754)

The King's Old Courtier:
When mighty roast beef was the Englishman's food,
It ennobled our hearts, and enriched our blood,
Our soldiers were brave, and our courtiers were good.
Oh the roast beef of Old England,
And Old England's roast beef!

But since we have learnt from all-conquering France,
To eat their ragouts as well as to dance,
Oh what a fine figure we make in romance!
Oh the roast beef of Old England,
And Old England's roast beef!

The Delicacies of English-speaking Countries

From *In Defence of English Cooking, 1945*

George Orwell (1903–1950)

It is commonly said, even by the English themselves, that English cooking is the worst in the world. It is supposed to be not merely incompetent, but also imitative, and I even read quite recently, in a book by a French writer, the remark: 'The best English cooking is, of course, simply French cooking.'

Now that is simply not true, as anyone who has lived long abroad will know, there is a whole host of delicacies which it is quite impossible to obtain outside the English-speaking countries. No doubt the list could be added to, but here are some of the things that I myself have sought for in foreign countries and failed to find.

First of all, kippers, Yorkshire pudding, Devonshire cream, muffins and crumpets. Then a list of puddings that would be interminable if I gave it in full: I will pick out for special mention Christmas pudding, treacle tart and apple dumplings. Then an almost equally long list of cakes: for instance, dark plum cake (such as you used to get at Buzzard's before the war), short-bread and saffron buns. Also innumerable kinds of biscuit, which exist, of course, elsewhere, but are generally admitted to be better and crisper in England.

Then there are the various ways of cooking potatoes that are peculiar to our own country. Where else do you see potatoes roasted under the joint, which is far and away the best way of cooking them? Or the delicious potato cakes that you get in the north of England? And it is far better to cook new potatoes in the English way – that is, boiled with mint and then served with a little melted butter or margarine – than to fry them as is done in most countries.

Then there are the various sauces peculiar to England. For instance, bread sauce, horse-radish sauce, mint sauce and apple sauce; not to mention redcurrant jelly, which is excellent with mutton as well as with hare, and various kinds of sweet pickle, which we seem to have in greater profusion than most countries.

What else? Outside these islands I have never seen a haggis, except one that came out of a tin, nor Dublin prawns, nor Oxford marmalade, nor several other kinds of jam (marrow jam and bramble jelly, for instance), nor sausages of quite the same kind as ours.

Then there are the English cheeses. There are not many of them but I fancy Stilton is the best cheese of its type in the world, with Wensleydale not far behind. English apples are also outstandingly good, particularly the Cox's Orange Pippin.

And finally, I would like to put in a word for English bread. All the bread is good, from the enormous Jewish loaves flavoured with caraway seeds to the Russian rye bread which is the colour of black treacle. Still, if there is anything quite as good as the soft part of the crust from an English cottage loaf (how soon shall we be seeing cottage loaves again?) I do not know of it.

No doubt some of the things I have named above could be obtained in continental Europe, just as it is possible in London to obtain vodka or bird's nest soup. But they are all native to our shores, and over huge areas they are literally unheard of.

French and American Eating Habits

From *In Defence of Food, 2008* | Michael Pollan (1955–)

The French eat very differently than we do. They seldom snack, and they eat most of their food at meals shared with other people. They eat small portions and don't come back for seconds. And they spend considerably more time eating than we do. Taken together, these habits contribute to a food culture in which the French consume fewer calories than we do, yet manage to enjoy them far more.

Taste

From *The Physiology of Taste, 1825*

Jean Anthelme Brillat-Savarin (1755–1826)

Translated by Fayette Robinson, 1854

Taste may be considered in three relations.

In physical man it is the apparatus by means of which he appreciates flavours.
In moral man it is the sensation which the organ impressed by any savorous centre impresses on the common centre. Considered as a material cause, taste is the property which a body has to impress the organ and to create a sensation.

Taste seems to have two chief uses:

1. It invites us by pleasure to repair the losses which result from the use of life.

2. It assists us to select from among the substances offered by nature, those which are alimentary.

Eyeing Gingerbread

From *Emma, 1815* | Jane Austen (1775–1817)

Observed in Highbury:
A string of dawdling children round the baker's little bow-window
eyeing the gingerbread.

Pease Porridge

Traditional English Nursery Rhyme

Pease Porridge hot,
Pease Porridge cold,
Pease Porridge in the pot
Nine days old.

Some like it hot,
Some like it cold,
Some like it in the pot
Nine days old.

23 February

Burnt Porridge

From *Jane Eyre, 1847* | Charlotte Brontë (1816–1855)

The refectory was a great, low-ceiled, gloomy room; on two long tables smoked basins of something hot, which, however, to my dismay, sent forth an odour far from inviting. I saw a universal manifestation of discontent when the fumes of the repast met the nostrils of those destined to swallow it; from the van of the procession, the tall girls of the first class, rose the whispered words –

'Disgusting! The porridge is burnt again!'

. . . .

Ravenous, and now very faint, I devoured a spoonful or two of my portion without thinking of its taste; but the first edge of hunger blunted, I perceived I had got in hand a nauseous mess; burnt porridge is almost as bad as rotten potatoes; famine itself soon sickens over it. The spoons were moved slowly: I saw each girl taste her food and try to swallow it; but in most cases the effort was soon relinquished. Breakfast was over, and none had breakfasted. Thanks being returned for what we had not got, and a second hymn chanted, the refectory was evacuated for the schoolroom. I was one of the last to go out, and in passing the tables, I saw one teacher take a basin of the porridge and taste it; she looked at the others; all their countenances expressed displeasure, and one of them, the stout one, whispered –

'Abominable stuff! How shameful!'

Porridge with Treacle

From *The Secret Garden, 1911* | Frances Hodgson Burnett (1849–1924)

A table in the centre was set with a good substantial breakfast. But she had always had a very small appetite, and she looked with something more than indifference at the first plate Martha set before her.

'I don't want it,' she said.

'Tha' doesn't want thy porridge!' Martha exclaimed incredulously.

'No.'

'Tha' doesn't know how good it is. Put a bit o' treacle on it or a bit o' sugar.'

'I don't want it,' repeated Mary.

'Eh!' said Martha. 'I can't abide to see good victuals go to waste. If our children was at this table they'd clean it bare in five minutes.'

'Why?' said Mary coldly.

'Why!' echoed Martha. 'Because they scarce ever had their stomachs full in their lives. They're as hungry as young hawks an' foxes.'

'I don't know what it is to be hungry,' said Mary, with the indifference of ignorance.

. . . .

But after a few days spent almost entirely out of doors she wakened one morning knowing what it was to be hungry, and when she sat down to her breakfast she did not glance disdainfully at her porridge and push it away, but took up her spoon and began to eat it and went on eating it until her bowl was empty.

'Tha' got on well enough with that this mornin', didn't tha'?' said Martha.

'It tastes nice today' said Mary, feeling a little surprised herself.

Rules to be Observed in Making Puddings, &c.

From *The Art of Cookery Made Plain and Easy, 1747*

Hannah Glasse (1708–1770)

In boiled Puddings, take great Care the Bag or Cloth be very clean, not soapy, but dipped in hot Water, and then well flowered. If a Bread-pudding, tye it loose; if a Batter-pudding, tye it close; and be sure the Water bolis when you put the Pudding in, and you should move the Puddings in the Pot now and then, for fear they stick. When you make a Batter-pudding, first mix the Flour well with a little Milk, then put in the Ingredients by degrees, and it will be smooth and not have Lumps; but for a plain Batter-pudding, the best way is to strain it through a coarse Hair Sieve, that it may either have Lumps, nor the Treadels of the Eggs: And all other Puddings, strain the Eggs when they are beat. If you boil them in Wooden-bowls, or China-dishes, butter the Inside before you put in your Batter: And all baked Puddings, butter the Pan or Dish, before the Pudding is put in.

Making Tom Kitten into a Dumpling Roly-poly Pudding

From *The Tale of Samuel Whiskers, 1908* | Beatrix Potter (1866–1943)

Presently the rats came back and set to work to make him into a dumpling. First they smeared him with butter, and then they rolled him in the dough.

'Will not the string be very indigestible, Anna Maria?' inquired Samuel Whiskers.

Anna Maria said she thought that it was of no consequence; but she wished that Tom Kitten would hold his head still, as it disarranged the pastry. She laid hold of his ears.

Tom Kitten bit and spat, and mewed and wriggled; and the rolling-pin went roly-poly, roly; roly, poly, roly. The rats each held an end.

'His tail is sticking out! You did not fetch enough dough, Anna Maria.'

'I fetched as much as I could carry,' replied Anna Maria.

'I do not think'– said Samuel Whiskers, pausing to take a look at Tom Kitten – 'I do *not* think it will be a good pudding. It smells sooty.'

Pastries, Sweets and Cakes

From *A Handbook of Cookery for a Small House, 1923*

Jessie Conrad (1873–1936)

For Tarts the fruit of all kinds must always be cooked first by itself. Bottled fruits should also be brought to a boil with sugar before being put into the pastry, except for baked apple dumplings.

For Puddings the fruit should not be cooked before. Suet crust should be mixed with water with just the chill off but not hot.

Milk puddings always require to be cooked in a very slow oven.

Never use brown sugar for sweetening except for Christmas pudding and apple pudding.

A Fairy Feast

From *The Enchanted Castle, 1907*

E. Nesbit (1858–1924)

It was not a silver tray, as you might have expected, but an oblong tin one. She set it down noisily on the end of the long table and breathed a sigh of relief.

'Oh! it *was* heavy,' she said. I don't know what fairy feast the children's fancy had been busy with. Anyhow, this was nothing like it. The heavy tray held a loaf of bread, a lump of cheese, and a brown jug of water. The rest of its heaviness was just plates and mugs and knives.

'Come along,' said the princess hospitably. 'I couldn't find anything but bread and cheese – but it doesn't matter, because everything's magic here, and unless you have some dreadful secret fault the bread and cheese will turn into anything you like. What *would* you like?' she asked Kathleen.

'Roast chicken,' said Kathleen, without hesitation.

The pinky princess cut a slice of bread and laid it on a dish. 'There you are,' she said, 'roast chicken. Shall I carve it, or will you?'

'You, please,' said Kathleen, and received a piece of dry bread on a plate.

'Green peas?' asked the Princess, cut a piece of cheese and laid it beside the bread.

Kathleen began to eat the bread, cutting it up with knife and fork as you would eat chicken. It was no use owning that she didn't see any chicken and peas, or anything but cheese and dry bread, because that would be owning that she had some dreadful secret fault.

'If I have, it *is* a secret, even from me,' she told herself.

MARCH

A Dinner of Fifty Dishes

Interesting Shapes

From *Gulliver's Travels: A Voyage to Laputa, 1726* |

Jonathan Swift (1667–1745)

My Dinner was brought, and four Persons of Quality, whom I
remembered to have seen very near the King's Person, did me the
Honour to dine with me. We had two Courses, of three Dishes
each. In the first Course, there was a Shoulder of Mutton, cut into
an Æquilateral Triangle, a Piece of Beef into a Rhomboides; and a
Pudding into a Cycloid. The second Course was two Ducks trussed
up in the Form of Fiddles; Sausages and Puddings resembling Flutes
and Haut-boys, and a Breast of Veal in the Shape of a Harp. The
Servants cut our Bread into Cones, Cylinders, Parallelograms, and
several other Mathematical Figures.

Signs of the Zodiac

From *The Satyricon, c. AD 63–65* | Petronius (AD 27–66)

Translated by William Burnaby (1673–1706)

Supplements of this translation were later proved to be spurious.

The novelty of the thing drew every man's eye upon it; it was a large
charger, with the twelve signs round it; upon every one of which the
master cook had laid somewhat or other suitable to the sign. Upon
Aries, chick-pease, (a pulse not unlike a ram's head); upon Taurus a
piece of beef; upon Gemini a pair of pendulums and kidneys; upon
Cancer a coronet; upon Leo an African figg; upon Virgo, a well-
grown boy; upon Libra a pair of scales, in one of which was a tart,
in the other a custard; upon Scorpio a pilchard; upon Sagittary a
grey-hound; upon Capricorn a lobster; upon Aquarius a goose; upon
Pisces two mullets; and in the middle a plat of herbs, cut out like a
green turf, and over them a honey-comb.

The Accusation

From *Alice's Adventures in Wonderland*, 1865 |

Lewis Carroll (1832–1898)

'Herald, read the accusation!' said the King.
On this the White Rabbit blew three blasts on the trumpet, and then
unrolled the parchment scroll, and read as follows:–

'The Queen of Hearts, she made some tarts,
    All on a summer day:
The Knave of Hearts, he stole those tarts,
    And took them quite away!'

Bachelors Entertaining

From *Kitchen Essays, 1922* | Agnes Jekyll (1861–1937)

Let us picture a bachelor living in a modest London house or in country surroundings close to his work, with a married couple, or oftener a working housekeeper, to look after him. Being constantly entertained by his friends and relations, he naturally desires occasionally to offer something in return: Problems of hospitality for such are oftenest solved by inviting their friends to a restaurant dinner or play – an agreeable but expensive solution – or by invitation cards for luncheons or teas at some race meeting or popular cricket match, when all responsibility is taken over by the club or contractor. This sort of entertaining, however, welcome as it may often be, seems to lack the personal note, for we do not really know our friends until we can visualize them in their own surroundings, and take an interest in the gathered treasures or the pursuits of their homes. A host, moreover, feels and appears at a greater advantage by his own fireside than in the garish setting of a public restaurant.

. . . .

The dictum of an eminent Victorian housekeeper still holds: 'Give your friends what you have yourselves; only have enough of it, and make it a little nicer.'

4 March

Menu for a Late Supper

From *Simple French Cooking for English Homes*, 1923

Xavier Marcel Boulestin (1878–1943)

AFTER AN INFORMAL PARTY

Soupe aux choix
Mixed cold meats
Salad
Dessert coffee

Nothing better, say at 3 o'clock in the morning, than a boiling hot *soupe au choix* and cold meat, with a very fresh, crisp salad. And you should drink with this one of those little white or pink wines from Anjou or Touraine, which have such a pleasant, sharp taste. Strong, black coffee on top of it and you will feel ready to start again, whatever you may have been doing, or walk home all the way.

This is more suitable, though, for Chelsea than Bayswater – unless the inhabitants of this 'highly desirable district' happen to feel, for once, 'delightfully Bohemian'.

Drinking

From *Anacreontics, 1656* | Abraham Cowley (1618–1667)

The thirsty earth soaks up the rain,
And drinks and gapes for drink again;
The plants suck in the earth, and are
With constant drinking fresh and fair;
The sea itself, which one would think
Should have but little need of drink,
Drinks ten thousand rivers up,
So filled that they o'erflow the cup.
The busy sun – and one would guess
By 's drunken fiery face no less –
Drinks up the sea, and when he 'as done,
The moon and stars drink up the sun;
They drink and dance by their own light,
They drink and revel all the night.
Nothing in Nature 's sober found,
But an eternal health goes round.
Fill up the bowl, then, fill it high!
Fill all the glasses there! for why
Should every creature drink but I?
Why, man of morals? tell me why!

Paan

From *Dishoom, 2019* |

Shamil Thakrar (1971–), Kavi Thakrar (1982–) and Naved Nasir (1979–)

Chowpatty is also an excellent place to try some *paan*. These are the fragrant parcels you'll have seen being sold from shops and street stalls all over Bombay. A betel leaf is packed with grated coconut, gulkand (a preserve of rose petals), candied fennel seeds and dried fruits, all neatly folded up, popped in the mouth, and chewed vigorously. The red spatters across the pavements and walls are the consequence of the traditional variety, which contains betel nut and sometimes tobacco and which needs to be spat out. Avoid these more pernicious components. You should only try the *meethe* (sweet) *paan*.

There's one stall in particular that has a fantastic keeper, Sharma Paanwala. He sports a long, lustrously waxed and well-groomed moustache. Visit him, place your order, and he'll assemble your neat parcel in seconds. From the speed at which his hands move while he twinkles his eyes at you, it's obvious to you that he'd be able to do this blindfolded whilst reciting Sanskrit scriptures. Then, without any hesitation or much warning, he deftly pops the *paan* into your mouth, which is somehow open and ready. It's an acquired taste: not just the food itself, but also being hand-fed in this way by a grown man who is not your mother. No matter. Embrace it. Ignore any urge to spit. Chew upon the *paan* as it releases its delightful flavours and freshens your mouth. You may or may not agree that they are delightful flavours but it's an experience either way.

The Maltster

From *Far from the Madding Crowd*, 1874 |

Thomas Hardy (1840–1928)

The maltster, after having lain down in his clothes for a few
hours, was now sitting beside a three-legged table, breakfasting off
bread and bacon. This was eaten on the plateless system, which is
performed by placing a slice of bread upon the table, the meat flat
upon the bread, a mustard plaster upon the meat, and a pinch of salt
upon the whole, then cutting them vertically downwards with a large
pocket-knife till wood is reached, when the severed lump is impaled
on the knife, elevated, and sent the proper way of food. The maltster's
lack of teeth appeared not to sensibly diminish his powers as a mill.
He had been without them for so many years that toothlessness
was felt less to be a defect than hard gums an acquisition. Indeed,
he seemed to approach the grave as a hyperbolic curve approaches a
straight line – less directly as he got nearer, till it was doubtful if he
would ever reach it at all.

No Excuse

From *The Chronicles of Clovis: The Match-Maker, 1911*

Saki / H. H. Munro (1870–1916)

Clovis approached the supper-table:

'I'm starving,' he announced, making an effort to sit down gracefully and read the menu at the same time.

'So I gathered;' said his host, 'from the fact that you were nearly punctual. I ought to have told you that I'm a Food Reformer. I've ordered two bowls of bread-and-milk and some health biscuits. I hope you don't mind.'

Clovis pretended afterwards that he didn't go white above the collar-line for the fraction of a second.

'All the same,' he said, 'you ought not to joke about such things. There really are such people. I've known people who've met them. To think of all the adorable things there are to eat in the world, and then to go through life munching sawdust and being proud of it.'

'They're like the Flagellants of the Middle Ages, who went about mortifying themselves.'

'They had some excuse,' said Clovis. 'They did it to save their immortal souls, didn't they? You needn't tell me that a man who doesn't love oysters and asparagus and good wines has got a soul, or a stomach either. He's simply got the instinct for being unhappy highly developed.'

Too Much Luxury

From *The Turkish Embassy Letters, 1763*

Lady Mary Wortley Montagu (1689–1762)

Pera, Constantinople
10 March, 1718
To Lady Mar

Dinner with the Sultana Hafise:
She gave me a dinner of fifty dishes of meat, which, after their
fashion, were placed on the table but one at a time, and was
extremely tedious. But the magnificence of her table answered very
well to that of her dress. The knives were of gold, the hafts set with
diamonds, but the piece of luxury which grieved my eyes was the
tablecloth and napkins, which were all tiffany, embroidered with silk
and gold, in the finest manner in natural flowers. It was with the
utmost regret that I made use of these costly napkins, which were
as finely wrought as the finest handkerchiefs that ever came out of
this country. You may be sure that they were entirely spoiled before
dinner was over. The sherbet, which is the liquor they drink at meals,
was served in china bowls, but the covers and salvers massy gold.
After dinner water was brought in a gold basin and towels of the same
kind with the napkins, which I very unwillingly wiped my hands
upon, and coffee was served in china, with gold soûcoupes [saucers].

How to Eat Rather Than How to Cook

From *How to Eat, 1998* | Nigella Lawson (1960–)

Although it's possible to love eating without being able to cook, I don't believe you can ever really cook unless you love eating. Such love, of course, is not something that can be taught, but it can be conveyed – and maybe that's the point. In writing this book I wanted to make food and my slavering passion for it the starting point; indeed for me it was the starting point. I have nothing to declare but my greed.

The French, who've lost something of their culinary confidence in recent years, remain solid on this front. Some years ago in France, in response to the gastronomic apathy and consequent lowering of standards nationally – what is known as *la crise* – Jack Lang, then Minister of Culture instituted *la semaine du goût*. He set up a body expressly to go into schools and other institutions not to teach anyone how to cook, but how to eat. This group might take with it a perfect baguette, an exquisite cheese, some local specialty cooked *comme il faut*, some fruit and vegetables grown properly and picked when ripe, in the belief that if the pupils, if people generally, tasted what was good, what was right, they would respect these traditions; by eating good food, they would want to cook. And so the cycle continues.

Refreshment Bar

From *Dubliners: Two Gallants, 1914* | James Joyce (1882–1941)

He [Lenehan] paused at last before the window of a poor-looking shop over which the words *Refreshment Bar* were printed in white letters. On the glass of the window were two flying inscriptions: *Ginger Beer* and *Ginger Ale*. A cut ham was exposed on a great blue dish while near it on a plate lay a segment of very light plum-pudding. He eyed this food earnestly for some time and then, after glancing warily up and down the street, went into the shop quickly.

He was hungry for, except some biscuits which he had asked two grudging curates to bring him, he had eaten nothing since breakfast-time. He sat down at an uncovered wooden table opposite two work-girls and a mechanic. A slatternly girl waited on him.

'How much is a plate of peas?' he asked.

'Three halfpence, sir,' said the girl.

'Bring me a plate of peas,' he said, 'and a bottle of ginger beer.'

He spoke roughly in order to belie his air of gentility for his entry had been followed by a pause of talk. His face was heated. To appear natural he pushed his cap back on his head and planted his elbows on the table. The mechanic and the two work-girls examined him point by point before resuming their conversation in a subdued voice. The girl brought him a plate of grocer's hot peas, seasoned with pepper and vinegar, a fork and his ginger beer. He ate his food greedily and found it so good that he made a note of the shop mentally. When he had eaten all the peas he sipped his ginger beer.

French Cooking

From *Mastering the Art of French Cooking, Volume One, 1961* |
Julia Child (1912–2004), Louisette Bertholle (1905–1999), Simone Beck (1904–1991)

All the techniques employed in French cooking are aimed at one goal: how does it taste? The French are seldom interested in unusual combinations or surprise presentations. With an enormous background of traditional dishes to choose from (*1000 Ways to Prepare and Serve Eggs* is the title of one French book on the subject) the Frenchman takes his greatest pleasure from a well known dish impeccably cooked and served. A perfect *navarin* of lamb, for instance, requires a number of operations including brownings, simmerings, strainings, skimmings and flavourings. Each of the several steps in the process, though simple to accomplish, plays a critical role, and if any is eliminated or combined with another, the texture and taste of the *navarin* suffer. One of the main reasons that pseudo-French cooking, with which we are all too familiar, falls far below good French cooking is just this matter of elimination of steps, combination of processes, or skimping on ingredients such as butter, cream – and time. 'Too much trouble', 'Too expensive', or 'Who will know the difference' are death knells for good food.

Cooking is not a particularly difficult art, and the more you cook and learn about cooking, the more sense it makes. But like any art it requires practice and experience. The most important ingredient you can bring to it is love of cooking for its own sake.

13 March

The Pat of Butter

Thomas Hardy (1840–1928)

Once, at the Agricultural Show,
    We tasted – all so yellow –
      Those butter-pats, cool and mellow!
Each taste I still remember, though
    It was so long ago.

This spoke of the grass of Netherhay,
    And this of Kingcomb Hill,
      And this of Coker Rill:
Which was the prime I could not say
    Of all those tried that day,

Till she, the fair and wicked-eyed,
    Held out a pat to me:
      Then felt I all Yeo-Lea
Was by her sample sheer outvied;
    And, 'This is the best,' I cried.

The Golden Age of Butter in English Cookery

From *Historic Heston, 2013* | Heston Blumenthal (1966–)

Some seventeenth- and eighteenth-century chefs took their enthusiasm for this new ingredient too far. Now that they had recognized butter's potential, they put it in everything, and lots of it. The French diplomat Talleyrand's famous observation 'that England has three sauces and 360 religions, whereas France has three religions and 360 sauces' was supposedly prompted by the ubiquity of butter sauce on English tables. However, it wasn't only foreigners who thought English cooks had gone overboard for butter. In his diary entry for 17 October 1756, Sussex shopkeeper Thomas Turner complained that dinner at his uncle's was 'spoiled by almost swimming in butter ... there was almost but enough in it to have drowned the pig, had it been alive'. Although the fact that his uncle risked serving a butter pond pudding after roast pig and turnips dressed in butter suggests a fairly devil-may-care approach to menu planning in any case.

Rôti sans Pareil

From *Venus in the Kitchen: or Love's Cookery Book, 1952*

Norman Douglas (1868–1952)

Take a large olive, stone it and stuff it with a paste made of anchovy,
 capers and oil.

Put the olive inside a trussed and boned bec-figue (garden warbler).

Put the bec-figue inside a fat ortolan.

Put the ortolan inside a boned lark.

Put the stuffed lark inside a boned thrush.

Put the thrush inside a fat quail.

Put the quail, wrapped in vine leaves, inside a boned lapwing.

Put the lapwing inside a boned plover.

Put the plover inside a fat, boned, red-legged partridge.

Put the partridge inside a young, boned, and well-hung woodcock.

Put the woodcock, rolled in breadcrumbs, inside a boned teal.

Put the teal inside a boned guinea-fowl.

Put the guinea-fowl, well larded inside a young and boned
 tame duck.

Put the duck inside a boned and fat fowl.

Put the fowl inside a well hung pheasant.

Put the pheasant inside a boned and fat wild goose.

Put the goose inside a fine turkey.

Put the turkey inside a boned bustard.

Having arranged your roast after this fashion, place it in a saucepan of proper size with onions stuffed with cloves, carrots, small squares of ham, celery, mignonette, several strips of bacon well seasoned, pepper, salt, spice, coriander seeds, and two cloves of garlic.

Seal the saucepan hermetically by closing it with pastry. Then put it for ten hours over a gentle fire and arrange it so that the heat penetrates evenly. An oven moderately heated would suit better than the hearth.

Before serving, remove the pastry, put your roast on a hot dish after having removed the grease, if there is any, and serve.

. . . .

(Abbreviated from *Le Parfait Cuisinier* of A. T. Raimbault, 1814.) It might be difficult to procure so varied an assortment of wild fowls anywhere at one and the same time; difficult, too, to find bustards in Europe nowadays; difficult, too, to stuff a bigger bird like the lapwing into a smaller one like the plover. I observe with sorrow that the common partridge, one of the best of all game birds, is not represented in this aviary.

Reasons for Drinking

Traditional Irish Rhyme

There are many good reasons for drinking,
And one has just entered my head.
If a man doesn't drink when he's living
How in the hell can he drink when he's dead?

The Cocktail Party

From *The Constance Spry Cookery Book, 1956*

Constance Spry (1886–1960) and Rosemary Hume (1907–1984)

Chapter 1

Perhaps a cookery book should start in a less frivolous fashion than with a chapter headed 'The Cocktail Party,' and should show in its initial stages a proper seriousness of purpose and general sober-mindedness. But I had an idea that perhaps a light-hearted approach might present a more immediate appeal. One never knows, indeed, what trifle may awaken the enthusiasm necessary to carry one beyond the early arduous tasks connected with cooking into those realms in which cookery is an art and a pleasure. Rosemary Hume and I have noticed that a lesson or demonstration on cocktail savouries is always popular, conjuring up as it does a vista of successful parties to be held in the future, and imparting a touch of glamour to the basic realities of the kitchen. Well, if the desire to excel in making good bouchées encourages a student to achieve mastery with pastry, all is well. Maybe this chapter should be regarded as the jam with the powder, the carrot before the donkey, but no matter if it serves to lure anyone into the kitchen. It is only fair to admit that neither R. H. nor I set great store by cocktails or their accompanying savouries, regarding them, as it were, as menaces to the appreciation of food.

18 March

100

Madeleines

From *Remembrance of Things Past: Du côté de chez Swann,
1913 (France), Swann's Way, 1922 (UK)* | Marcel Proust (1871–1922)

Translated by C. K. Scott Moncrieff (1889–1930)

Ouverture

And suddenly the memory returns. The taste was that of the little
crumb of madeleine which on Sunday mornings at Combray
(because on those mornings I did not go out before church-time),
when I went to say good day to her in her bedroom my aunt Léonie
used to give me, dipping it first in her own cup of real or of lime-
flower tea. The sight of the little madeleine had recalled nothing to
my mind before I tasted it; perhaps because I had so often seen such
things in the interval, without tasting them, on the trays in pastry-
cooks' windows, that their image had dissociated itself from those
Combray days to take its place among others more recent; perhaps
because of those memories, so long abandoned and put out of mind,
nothing now survived, everything was scattered; the forms of things,
including that of the little scallop-shell of pastry, so richly sensual
under its severe, religious folds, were either obliterated or had been
so long dormant as to have lost the power of expansion which would
have allowed them to resume their place in my consciousness. But
when from a long-distant past nothing subsists, after the people are
dead, after the things are broken and scattered, still, alone, more
fragile, but with more vitality, more unsubstantial, more persistent,
more faithful, the smell and taste of things remain poised a long
time, like souls, ready to remind us, waiting and hoping for their
moment, amid the ruins of all the rest; and bear unfaltering, in the

tiny and almost impalpable drop of their essence, the vast structure of recollection.

And once I had recognised the taste of the crumb of madeleine soaked in her decoction of lime-flowers which my aunt used to give me (although I did not yet know and must long postpone the discovery of why this memory made me so happy) immediately the old grey house upon the street, where her room was, rose up like the scenery of a theatre to attach itself to the little pavilion, opening on to the garden, which had been built out behind it for my parents (the isolated panel which until that moment had been all that I could see); and with the house the town, from morning to night and in all weathers, the Square where I was sent before luncheon, the streets along which I used to run errands, the country roads we took when it was fine. And just as the Japanese amuse themselves by filling a porcelain bowl with water and steeping in it little crumbs of paper which until then are without character or form, but, the moment they become wet, stretch themselves and bend, take on colour and distinctive shape, become flowers or houses or people, permanent and recognisable, so in that moment all the flowers in our garden and in M. Swann's park, and the water-lilies on the Vivonne and the good folk of the village and their little dwellings and the parish church and the whole of Combray and of its surroundings, taking their proper shapes and growing solid, sprang into being, town and gardens alike, from my cup of tea.

Reminiscences of Good Cheer

From *The Scarlet Letter, 1850* | Nathaniel Hawthorne (1804–1864)

The Inspector at the Customs-House:

His reminiscences of good cheer, however ancient the date of the actual banquet, seemed to bring the savor of pig or turkey under one's very nostrils. There were flavors on his palate that had lingered there not less than sixty or seventy years, and were still apparently as fresh as that of the mutton-chop which he had just devoured for his breakfast. I have heard him smack his lips over dinners, every guest at which, except himself, had long been food for worms. It was marvellous to observe how the ghosts of bygone meals were continually rising up before him; not in anger or retribution, but as if grateful for his former appreciation and seeking to resuscitate an endless series of enjoyment, at once shadowy and sensual. A tenderloin of beef, a hind-quarter of veal, a spare-rib of pork, a particular chicken, or a remarkably praiseworthy turkey, which had perhaps adorned his board in the days of the elder Adams, would be remembered; while all the subsequent experience of our race, and all the events that brightened or darkened his individual career, had gone over him with as little permanent effect as the passing breeze. The chief tragic event of the old man's life, so far as I could judge, was his mishap with a certain goose which lived and died some twenty or forty years ago; a goose of most promising figure, but which, at table, proved so inveterately tough that the carving-knife would make no impression on its carcass, and it could only be divided with an axe and handsaw.

A Cube is Only the Root

From *Freud on Food, 1978* | Clement Freud (1924–2009)

It is a sobering thought that if you chop an onion, a carrot and some celery; brown them gently in oil; add a pound of shin of beef; a handful of marrowbones, a bayleaf, seasoning and two quarts of water; then simmer the lot for 2 hours, the end product will not be noticeably nicer than Knorr Suisse soup cubes dissolved in boiling water. The trouble about serving the unadulterated juice of a soup cube is that, while it makes an adequate consommé, it makes no more than that. It is also instantly recognizable and serving it neat will do astonishingly little for your standing as a great host or hostess.

The right use for soup-stock – whether ponderously manufactured or instantly produced – is as a basis. You start with the all-purpose liquid, then set about giving it an identity, an added strength and some character. Start by remembering the enigma of soup-making: small saucepanfuls always turn out better than very large quantities, even if all the ingredients are carefully multiplied the requisite number of times.

Barometer Soup

From *A Tramp Abroad, 1880* | Mark Twain (1835–1910)

Our distresses being at an end, I now determined to rest the men in camp and give the scientific department of the Expedition a chance. First, I made a barometric observation, to get our altitude, but I could not perceive that there was any result. I knew, by my scientific reading, that either thermometers or barometers ought to be boiled, to make them accurate; I did not know which it was, so I boiled them both. There was still no result; so I examined these instruments and discovered that they possessed radical blemishes: the barometer had no hand but the brass pointer and the ball of the thermometer was stuffed with tin-foil. I might have boiled those things to rags, and never found out anything.

I hunted up another barometer; it was new and perfect. I boiled it half an hour in a pot of bean soup which the cooks were making. The result was unexpected: the instrument was not affected at all, but there was such a strong barometer taste to the soup that the head cook, who was a most conscientious person, changed its name in the bill of fare. The dish was so greatly liked by all, that I ordered the cook to have barometer soup every day.

Meat Without Mirth

Robert Herrick (1591–1674)

Eaten I have; and though I had good cheere,
I did not sup, because no friends were there.
Where Mirth and Friends are absent when we Dine
Or Sup, there wants the Incense and the Wine.

The Empire of the Tea-table

From *Lady Audley's Secret, 1862* | Mary Elizabeth Braddon (1835–1915)

Lucy Audley looked up from her occupation among the fragile china
cups and watched Robert rather anxiously as he walked softly to his
uncle's room and back again to the boudoir. She looked very pretty
and innocent, seated behind the graceful group of delicate opal china
and glittering silver. Surely a pretty woman never looks prettier
than when making tea. The most feminine and most domestic of
all occupations imparts a magic harmony to her every movement,
a witchery to her every glance. The floating mists from the boiling
liquid in which she infuses the soothing herbs; whose secrets are
known to her alone, envelope her in a cloud of scented vapour,
through which she seems a social fairy, weaving potent spells with
Gunpowder and Bohea. At the tea-table she reigns omnipotent,
unapproachable. What do men know of the mysterious beverage?
Read how poor Hazlitt made his tea, and shudder at the dreadful
barbarism. How clumsily the wretched creatures attempt to assist the
witch president of the tea-tray; how hopelessly they hold the kettle,
how continually they imperil the frail cups and saucers, or the taper
hands of the priestess. To do away with the tea-table is to rob woman
of her legitimate empire.

24 March

Stay at Home

From *The Bride of Lammermoor, 1819* | Sir Walter Scott (1771–1832)

Sir, stay at home and take an old man's counsel;
Seek not to bask you by a stranger's hearth;
Our own blue smoke is warmer than their fire,
Domestic food is wholesome, though 'tis homely,
And foreign dainties poisonous, though tasteful.

Beans

From *Good Things, 1971* | Jane Grigson (1928–1990)

Every civilization has its special beans. Europe's classical bean, back to the Greeks, was the broad bean. The bean of the Incas, and the Mexicans, was the kidney-bean, which Peruvian Indians were eating several thousand years ago.

When Europe obtained these new kidney-beans quite early in the sixteenth century, they were soon everybody's eating – especially dried, for winter food. It was the French, I think, and the Italians (so we say French bean, and used to say Roman bean) who devised most of the special bean dishes. Variously called haricot beans, butter beans, navy beans, Boston beans, the dried beans were haricots first of all because the French added them, with small turnips, to a haricot or ragoût of mutton.

Don't despise them. Beans may not be the pinnacle of Wine and Food Society living, but it is wonderful what can be made out of a packet of pallid, dull looking butter beans (from a variety whose pods are yellow or butter coloured) or the smaller haricot beans. It is wonderful how they combine without ceasing to be beans – particularly with olive oil. There is a basic marriage for you – if you like to mix history with your meals – of two civilizations, Andean and Mediterranean.

The Art of Cutting a Slice of Cold Beef

From *Lesley Castle, 1793* | Jane Austen (1775–1817)

Miss C. Lutterell to Miss M. Lesley

Bristol the 27th of March

I always longed particularly to go to Vaux-hall, to see whether
the cold Beef there is cut so thin as it is reported, for I have a sly
suspicion that few people understand the art of cutting a slice of
cold Beef so well as I do: nay it would be hard if I did not know
something of the Matter, for it was a part of my Education that
I took by far the most pains with.

27 March

Cutting Bread

From *Great Expectations, 1860–1861* | Charles Dickens (1812–1870)

My sister had a trenchant way of cutting our bread-and-butter for us, that never varied. First, with her left hand she jammed the loaf hard and fast against her bib – where it sometimes got a pin into it, and sometimes a needle, which we afterwards got into our mouths. Then she took some butter (not too much) on a knife and spread it on the loaf, in an apothecary kind of way, as if she were making a plaister, – using both sides of the knife with a slapping dexterity, and trimming and moulding the butter off round the crust. Then, she gave the knife a final smart wipe on the edge of the plaister, and then sawed a very thick round off the loaf: which she finally, before separating from the loaf, hewed into two halves, of which Joe got one, and I the other.

Preface to the First Edition

From *The Book of Household Management, 1861*

Mrs Isabella Beeton (1836–1865)

I must frankly own, that if I had known, beforehand, that this book would have cost me the labour which it has, I should never have been courageous enough to commence it. What moved me, in the first instance, to attempt a work like this, was the discomfort and suffering which I had seen brought upon men and women by household mismanagement. I have always thought that there is no more fruitful source of family discontent than a housewife's badly-cooked dinners and untidy ways. Men are now so well served out of doors, – at their clubs, well-ordered taverns, and dining-houses – that, in order to compete with the attractions of these places, a mistress must be thoroughly acquainted with the theory and practice of cookery, as well as be perfectly conversant with all the other arts of making and keeping a comfortable home.

A Better Book

From *The Life of Samuel Johnson, 1791* | James Boswell (1740–1795)

Samuel Johnson (1709–1784)

Samuel Johnson:

I could write a better book about cookery than has ever yet
been written; it should be a book upon philosophical principles.
Pharmacy is now made much more simple. Cookery may be so too.
A prescription, which is now compounded of five ingredients, had
formerly fifty in it. So in Cookery. If the nature of the ingredients is
well known, much fewer will do. Then, as you cannot make bad meat
good, I would tell you what is the best butcher's meat, the best beef,
the best pieces; how to choose young fowls; the proper seasons of
different vegetables; how to roast, and boil, and compound.

30 March

Pat-a-cake

Traditional English Nursery Rhyme

Pat-a-cake, pat-a-cake, baker's man,
Bake me a cake as fast as you can;
Pat it and prick it, and mark it with B,
Put it in the oven for Baby and me.

31 March

APRIL

A Basket of Sugar-cakes

Green Eggs and Ham

From *Green Eggs and Ham, 1960* | Dr Seuss (1904–1991)

I could not, would not, on a boat.
I will not, will not, with a goat.
I will not eat them in the rain.
I will not eat them on a train.
Not in the dark! Not in a tree!
Not in a car! You let me be!
I do not like them in a box.
I do not like them with a fox.
I will not eat them in a house.
I do not like them with a mouse.
I do not like them here or there.
I do not like them ANYWHERE!
I do not like green eggs and ham!
I do not like them, Sam-I-am.
You do not like them. So you say.
Try them! Try them! And you may.
Try them and you may, I say.
Sam!
If you let me be,
I will try them.
You will see.

(... And he tries them ...)
Sam!
I like green eggs and ham!
I do! I like them, Sam-I-am!
And I would eat them in a boat.
And I would eat them with a goat ...
And I will eat them, in the rain.
And in the dark. And on a train.
And in a car. And in a tree.
They are so good, so good, you see!
So I will eat them in a box.
And I will eat them with a fox.
And I will eat them in a house.
And I will eat them with a mouse.
And I will eat them here and there.
Say! I will eat them ANYWHERE!
I do so like green eggs and ham!
Thank you!
Thank you,
Sam-I-am!

1 April

Scones

From *Madhur Jaffrey's Cookbook: Food for Family and Friends, 1987* | Madhur Jaffrey (1933–)

To a teenager growing up in India, a scone seemed the most exotic of treats. It was so – well – foreign. Like tweeds, Wordsworth and the Royal Family, it was imbued with the aura of being quintessentially British. Even the way its name was pronounced – 'scon' – tickled me no end (I know now that it can be said two ways).

I ate scones very rarely in India. The first time I had one was in a houseboat moored on the Jhelum River in the mountainous state of Kashmir. There were only two of us living on that houseboat, both of us good friends on holiday, both seventeen and both studying English Literature at a woman's college in Delhi. If that sounds a bit daring for India in 1950, it wasn't really. Even though technically unchaperoned, we were guests of the state's Prime Minister.

Houseboats in Kashmir function as small, private hotels so the owner/chef of our three-bedroom affair was more than anxious to please us. We were fed four times a day and at each meal we were asked what we'd like for the next. *That* made us feel very grown-up. Many of the dishes offered were holdovers from colonial times when British families 'summered in the hills'. The foods that excited us the most were, quite naturally, the ones that were the farthest from our daily diet in the Plains. When the cook mentioned 'rhubarb' or 'asparagus', he sent us into a tizzy of excitement. And the day he asked if we would like scones for tea, we were practically hysterical with joyful anticipation. We could just see all those Bennet girls from *Pride and Prejudice* buttering their scones. Now *we* would do the same.

I liked the idea of a scone before I had the thing itself but once I'd taken my first bite of that crumbly, buttery delight, I was hooked for life.

Even today, my favourite tea consists of nothing more than freshly made scones washed down with 'the cup that cheers'. I serve this almost every other weekend to friends and family who visit us in the country.

What Did You Have for Dinner?

From *The Satyricon, c.* AD 63–65 | Petronius (AD 27–66)

Translated by William Burnaby (1673–1706)

Supplements of this translation were later proved to be spurious.

'But,' said Trimalchio, 'what had ye to eat?'

'I'll tell ye,' quoth Habinas, 'as near as I can, for my memory is not so good, but that sometimes I forget my own name: However, for the first dish we had a goodly porker, with a garland upon him, and puddings, goose giblets, lamb-stones, sweetbreads and gizzards round him; there were also beets and houshold-bread of his own baking, for himself, which I would rather have than white; it makes a man strong, and I never complain of what I like. The next was a cold tart, with excellent warm honey, and that Spanish, running upon it. I eat little of the tart; I tasted also the red pulse, and lupines, by the advice of Calvus, and several apples, of which I took away two in my handkerchief: for if I bring home nothing to my little she slave, I shall have snubs enough: this dame of mine puts me often in mind of her. We also had on a side-table a haunch of a bear, which Scintilla tasting ere she was aware, had like to have thrown up her guts: I on the other hand eat a pound of it or better, for me-thought it tasted like boars flesh; and I said, if a bear eats a man, why may not a man much more eat a bear? To be short, we had cream cheese, wine boil'd off to a third part, fry'd snails, chitterlings, livers, eggs, turneps, mustard, and a bowl that held a gallon. Don't disturb me, Palamedes; there were also handles about a basket of sugar-cakes, of which we wantonly took some, and sent away the gammon of bacon.

Bear / Ours

From *Le Grand Dictionnaire de la Cuisine, 1873* |

Alexandre Dumas (1802–1870)

Translated by Alan (1924–2003) and Jane (1927–2010) Davidson, 1978

There are few people of our generation who do not recall the sensation caused by the first installment of my *Impressions de Voyage* when people read the article 'Bear steak'. There was a universal outcry against the audacious narrator who dared to say that there were places in civilized Europe where bear is eaten.

It would have been easier to go to Chevet, and ask him if he had bear hams.

He would have enquired without a trace of surprise: 'Is it a Canadian leg or one from Transylvania which you wish?' And he could have furnished whichever he was asked for.

I could at that time have given to readers the advice which I give them today, but I took good care not to; there was a big commotion about the book, and since at that time I was just embarking on a literary career I could ask for nothing better.

But to my great astonishment, the person who should have been most pleased with the uproar, the innkeeper, de Martigny, was furious; he wrote to upbraid me, he wrote to the newspapers to get them to state in his name that he had never served bear to his travellers; but his fury kept increasing as each traveller asked him as their first question: 'Do you have any bear?'

If the stupid man had thought to answer yes, and then served ass, horsemeat or mule instead of bear, he would have made a fortune.

Since that time we have become more civilized; bear hams have become a dish one doesn't meet in every salted-provision dealer's premises, but which one can find without too much difficulty.

Enticing Titles

From *The Alice B. Toklas Cook Book, 1954*

Alice B. Toklas (1877–1967)

Bass for Picasso

Oeufs Francis Picabia

Gigot de la Clinique

Scheherazade's Melon

Nameless Cookies

Mutton Chops in Dressing-gowns

Omelette in an Overcoat

A Hen with Golden Eggs

Pink Pompadour Bass

Giant Squab in Pyjamas

Custard Josephine Baker

A Fine Fat Pullet

The Real Right Way for French Fried Potatoes

Bavarian Cream Perfect Love

Coco Marmalade

Swimming Crawfish

A Restricted Veal Loaf

Liberation Fruit Cake

Wedding Anniversary Ice Cream

Haschich Fudge

[The recipe for Haschich Fudge is on 11 December.]

5 April

Looking-Glass Cake

From *Through the Looking-Glass, 1871* | Lewis Carroll (1832–1898)

The Lion: 'What a time the Monster is, cutting up that cake!'

Alice had seated herself on the bank of a little brook, with the great dish on her knees, and was sawing away diligently with the knife. 'It's very provoking!' she said, in reply to the Lion (she was getting quite used to being called 'the Monster'). 'I've cut several slices already, but they always join on again!'

'You don't know how to manage Looking-glass cakes,' the Unicorn remarked. 'Hand it round first, and cut it afterwards.'

This sounded nonsense, but Alice very obediently got up, and carried the dish round, and the cake divided itself into three pieces as she did so.

'*Now* cut it up,' said the Lion, as she returned to her place with the empty dish.

6 April

A Hero

From *The Life of Samuel Johnson, 1791* | James Boswell (1740–1795)

Samuel Johnson (1709–1784)

7th April

Samuel Johnson:

Claret is the liquor for boys; port, for men; but he who aspires to be a hero (smiling) must drink brandy.

7 April

Wine and Water

G. K. Chesterton (1874–1936)

Old Noah he had an ostrich farm and fowls on the largest scale,
He ate his egg with a ladle in an egg-cup big as a pail,
And the soup he took was Elephant Soup and fish he took was Whale,
But they all were small to the cellar he took when he set out to sail,
And Noah he often said to his wife when he sat down to dine,
'I don't care where the water goes if it doesn't get into the wine.'

The cataract of the cliff of heaven fell blinding off the brink
As if it would wash the stars away as suds go down a sink,
The seven heavens came roaring down for the throats of hell to drink,
And Noah he cocked his eye and said, 'It looks like rain, I think,
The water has drowned the Matterhorn as deep as a Mendip mine,
But I don't care where the water goes if it doesn't get into the wine.'

But Noah he sinned, and we have sinned; on tipsy feet we trod,
Till a great big black teetotaller was sent to us for a rod,
And you can't get wine at a P.S.A., or chapel, or Eisteddfod,
For the Curse of Water has come again because of the wrath of God,
And water is on the Bishop's board and the Higher Thinker's shrine,
But I don't care where the water goes if it doesn't get into the wine.

A Special Dinner

From *The Road to Oxiana, 1937* | Robert Byron (1905–1941)

Maimena, Afghanistan

It will be a special dinner. A sense of well-being has come over us in this land of plenty. Basins of milk, pilau with raisins, skewered kabob well salted and peppered, plum jam, and new bread have already arrived from the bazaar; to which we have added some treats of our own, patent soup, tomato ketchup, prunes in gin, chocolate, and ovaltine. The whisky is lasting out well.

9 April

Now or After Tea

From *Peter and Wendy, 1911* | J. M. Barrie (1860–1937)

His courage was almost appalling. 'Do you want an adventure now,' he said casually to John, 'or would you like to have your tea first?'

Wendy said 'tea first' quickly, and Michael pressed her hand in gratitude, but the braver John hesitated.

'What kind of adventure?' he asked cautiously.

'There's a pirate asleep in the pampas just beneath us,' Peter told him. 'If you like, we'll go down and kill him.'

'I don't see him,' John said after a long pause.

'I do.'

'Suppose,' John said a little huskily, 'he were to wake up.'

Peter spoke indignantly. 'You don't think I would kill him while he was sleeping! I would wake him first, and then kill him. That's the way I always do.'

'I say! Do you kill many?'

'Tons.'

John said 'how ripping,' but decided to have tea first.

A Recipe for Civilisation

Thomas Hood (1799–1845)

Lines 1–26

Surely, those sages err who teach

That man is known from brutes by speech,

Which hardly severs man from woman,

But not th' inhuman from the human, –

Or else might parrots claim affinity,

And dogs be doctors by latinity, –

Not t' insist, (as might be shown)

That beasts have gibberish of their own,

Which once was no dead tongue, tho' we

Since Esop's days have lost the key;

Nor yet to hint dumb men, – and, still, not

Beasts that could gossip though they will not,

But play at dummy like the monkeys,

For fear mankind should make them flunkies.

Neither can man be known by feature

Or form, because so like a creature,

That some grave men could never shape

Which is the aped and which the ape,

Nor by his gait, nor by his height,

Nor yet because he's black or white,

But rational, – for so we call

The only COOKING ANIMAL!

The only one who brings his bit

Of dinner to the pot or spit,

For where's the lion e'er was hasty,

To put his ven'son in a pasty?

Gentlemen

From *The Anatomy of Melancholy, 1621* | Robert Burton (1577–1640)

A cook of old was a base knave (as Livy complains) but now is a great man in request: cookery is become an art: cooks are Gentlemen.

There was an Old Person of Ewell

Edward Lear (1812–1888)

There was an Old Person of Ewell,
Who chiefly subsisted on gruel;
But to make it more nice, he inserted some mice,
Which refreshed that Old Person of Ewell.

The Feast of the Calabashes

From *Typee, 1846* | Herman Melville (1819–1891)

All along the piazza of the Ti were arranged elaborately carved
canoe-shaped vessels, some twenty feet in length, filled with newly
made poee-poee, and sheltered from the sun by the broad leaves
of the banana. At intervals were heaps of green bread-fruit, raised
in pyramidical stacks, resembling the regular piles of heavy shot
to be seen in the yard of an arsenal. Inserted into the interstices of
the huge stones which formed the pi-pi were large boughs of trees;
hanging from the branches of which, and screened from the sun by
their foliage, were innumerable little packages with leafy coverings,
containing the meat of the numerous hogs which had been slain,
done up in this manner to make it more accessible to the crowd.
Leaning against the railing of the piazza were an immense number
of long, heavy bamboos, plugged at the lower end, and with their
projecting muzzles stuffed with a wad of leaves. These were filled
with water from the stream, and each of them might hold from
four to five gallons.

14 April

Piggs and Beer

From *The Diary of a Country Parson, 1778*

James Woodforde (1740–1803)

April 15

Brewed a vessel of strong Beer today. My two large Piggs, by
drinking some Beer grounds taking out of one of my Barrels today,
got so amazingly drunk by it, that they were not able to stand and
appeared like dead things almost, and so remained all night from
dinner time today. I never saw Piggs so drunk in my life …

April 16

… My 2 Piggs are still unable to walk yet, but they are better than
they were yesterday. They tumble about the yard and can by no
means stand at all steady yet. In the afternoon my 2 Piggs were
tolerably sober.

An Unpleasant Surprise

From *The Diary of a Nobody, 1892*

George Grossmith (1847–1912) and Weedon Grossmith (1854–1919)

April 16

When I had quite finished my supper, and was leaving, the waiter who had been attending on us arrested my attention by tapping me on the shoulder. I thought it unusual for a waiter at a private ball to expect a tip, but nevertheless gave a shilling, as he had been very attentive. He smilingly replied: 'I beg your pardon, sir, this is no good,' alluding to the shilling. 'Your party's had four suppers at 5s. a head, five ices at 1s., three bottles of champagne at 11s. 6d, a glass of claret, and a sixpenny cigar for the stout gentleman – in all £3 0s. 6d!'

I don't think I was ever so surprised in my life, and had only sufficient breath to inform him that I had received a private invitation, to which he answered that he was perfectly well aware of that; but that the invitation didn't include eatables and drinkables. A gentleman who was standing at the bar corroborated the waiter's statement, and assured me it was quite correct.

The waiter said he was extremely sorry if I had been under any misapprehension; but it was not his fault. Of course there was nothing to be done but to pay. So, after turning out my pockets, I just managed to scrape up sufficient, all but nine shillings; but the manager, on my giving my card to him, said: 'That's all right.'

I don't think I ever felt more humiliated in my life.

A Tactile Dinner Party

From *The Futurist Cookbook, 1932*

Filippo Tommaso Marinetti (1876–1944) and Fillìa (Luigi Colombo, 1904–1936)

Translated by Suzanne Brill (1932–2020)

The menu:

1. Polyrhythmic Salad: the waiters approach the tables carrying for each guest a box with a crank on the left side and, fixed half way up the right side, a china bowl. In the bowl: undressed lettuce leaves, dates and grapes. Without the help of cutlery, each diner uses his right hand to feed himself from the bowl while he turns the crank with his left. The box thus emits musical rhythms: and the waiters dance slowly with grand geometrical gestures in front of the tables until the food has been eaten.

2. Magic Food: this is served from smallish bowls covered on the outside with rough tactile materials. The bowl should be held in the left hand while the right is used to fish out mysterious balls it contains: these will all be made of caramel but each one filled with something different ingredients (such as candied fruits or bits of raw meat or mashed banana or chocolate or pepper.) so that the diners cannot guess which flavour will enter the mouth next.

3. Tactile Vegetable Garden: a large plate containing a wide variety of raw and cooked green vegetables without any dressing or sauce is placed in front of each guest. The greens can be nibbled at will but only by burying the face in the plate, without the help of the hands, so as to inspire a true tasting with direct contact between the flavours and textures of the green leaves on the skin of the cheeks and the lips. Every time the diners raise their heads to chew, the waiters spray their faces with perfumes of lavender and eau de Cologne.

Two Weevils

From *The Fortune of War, 1979* | Patrick O'Brian (1914–2000)

Two weevils crept from the crumbs. 'You see those weevils, Stephen?'
said Jack solemnly.

'I do.'

'Which would you choose?'

'There is not a scrap of difference. Arcades ambo. They are
the same species of curculio, and there is nothing to choose
between them.'

'But suppose you had to choose?'

'Then I should choose the right-hand weevil; it has a perceptible
advantage in both length and breadth.'

'There I have you,' cried Jack. 'You are bit – you are completely
dished. Don't you know that in the Navy you must always choose the
lesser of two weevils? Oh ha, ha, ha, ha!'

18 April

To Make Ketchup to Keep Twenty Years

From *The Art of Cookery Made Plain and Easy, 1747*

Hannah Glasse (1708–1770)

For Captains of Ships:

Take a Gallon of strong Stale Beer, one Pound of Anchovies washed from the Pickle, a Pound of Shallots, peeled, half an Ounce of Mace, half an Ounce of Cloves, a quarter of an Ounce of whole Pepper, three or four large Races of Ginger, two Quarts of the large Mushroom Flaps rubbed to Pieces. Cover all this close, and let it simmer till it is half wasted, then strain it through a Flannel Bag; let it stand till it is quite cold, then bottle it. You may carry it to the Indies, a Spoonful of this to a Pound of fresh Butter melted, makes a fine Fish Sauce. Or in the room of Gravy-Sauce, the stronger and staler the Beer is, the Better the Ketchup will be.

On Board a Boat Becalmed

From *Don Juan, Canto II, 1819* | George Gordon, Lord Byron (1788–1824)

LXVII

But man is a carnivorous production,
    And must have meals, at least one meal a day;
He cannot live, like woodcocks, upon suction,
    But, like the shark and tiger, must have prey;
Although his anatomical construction
    Bears vegetables, in a grumbling way,
Your labouring people think beyond all question,
Beef, veal, and mutton, better for digestion.

LXVIII

And thus it was with this our hapless crew;
    For on the third day there came on a calm,
And though at first their strength it might renew,
    And lying on their weariness like balm,
Lull'd them like turtles sleeping on the blue
    Of ocean, when they woke they felt a qualm,
And fell all ravenously on their provision,
Instead of hoarding it with due precision.

LXIX

The consequence was easily foreseen –
    They ate up all they had, and drank their wine,
In spite of all remonstrances, and then
    On what, in fact, next day were they to dine?
They hoped the wind would rise, these foolish men!
    And carry them to shore; these hopes were fine,
But as they had but one oar, and that brittle,
It would have been more wise to save their victual.

Chocolate Amber

From *The Physiology of Taste, 1825*

Jean Anthelme Brillat-Savarin (1755–1826)

Translated by Fayette Robinson, 1854

The Properties of Chocolate:
Now, then, let any man who has indulged too much in the cup of *volupté*; let every man who has passed in toil too much of the time when he should have slept; let every man of mind, who finds his faculties temporarily decay; every man who finds the air humid and the atmosphere painful to breathe; let every man who has a fixed idea which would deprive him of the liberty of thought; let them each take a *demi litre of chocolate ambré*, (sixty grains of amber to the kilogramme), and they will see wonders.

In my way of distinguishing things, I have called this *chocolate des affligés*; because in all the conditions I have referred to, there is something very like affliction.

21 April

.

Chocolate Drinks

From *The Cooks and Confectioners Dictionary, 1723*

John Nott (late 17th–early 18th century)

To make Chocolate with Water

To a Quart of Water, put a quarter of a Pound of Chocolate without Sugar, fine Sugar a quarter of a Pound, good Brandy a quarter of a Pound, fine Flour half a quarter of an Ounce, and a little Salt; mix them, dissolve them, and boil them; which will be done in ten or twelve Minutes.

To make Milk Chocolate

Take a Quart of Milk, Chocolate without Sugar four Ounces, fine Sugar as much, fine Flour or Starch, half a quarter of an Ounce, a little Salt; mix them, dissolve them, and boil them as before.

To make Wine Chocolate

Take a Pint of Sherry, or a Pint and a half of red Port, four Ounces and a half of Chocolate, six Ounces of fine Sugar, and half an Ounce of white Starch, or fine Flour; mix, dissolve, and boil all these as before. But if your Chocolate be with Sugar, take double the Quantity of Chocolate, and half the Quantity of Sugar; and so in all.

A Breakfast Ordered by a Hungry Man

From *Jack Abbott's Breakfast, 1847* | Leigh Hunt (1784–1859)

Jack Abbott plunges into the first coffee-house in sight:

'Waiter!'

'*Yessir,*'

'Breakfast immediately. Tea, black and green, and all that.'

'*Yessir.* Eggs and toast, sir?'

'By all means.'

'*Yessir,* Any ham, sir?'

'Just so, and instantly.'

'*Yessir.* Cold fowl, sir?'

'Precisely; and no delay.'

'*Yessir.* Anchovy perhaps, sir?'

'By all – eh ? – no, I don't care for anchovy – but pray bring what you like; and above all, make haste, my good fellow – no delay – I'm as hungry as the devil.'

'*Yessir* – coming directly, sir. ('Good chap and great fool,' said the waiter to himself.) 'Like the newspaper, sir?'

'Thankye. Now for Heaven's sake – '

'*Yessir* – immediately, sir – everything ready, sir.'

'Everything ready!' thought Jack. 'Cheering sound! Beautiful place a coffee-house! Fine *English* place – everything so snug and at hand – so comfortable – so easy – have what you like, and without fuss. What a breakfast I *shall* eat!

Ingredients

From *Book of Mediterranean Food, 1950* | Elizabeth David (1913–1992)

Preface to the Second Edition:

This book first appeared in 1950, when almost every essential ingredient of good cooking was either rationed or unobtainable. To produce the simplest meal consisting of two or even three genuine dishes required the utmost ingenuity and devotion. But even if people could not very often make the dishes here described, it was stimulating to think about them; to escape from the deadly boredom of queueing and the frustration of buying weekly rations; to read about real food cooked with wine and olive oil, eggs and butter and cream, and dishes richly flavoured with onions, garlic, herbs, and brightly coloured Southern vegetables.

. . . .

So startlingly different is the food situation now as compared with only two years ago that I think there is scarcely a single ingredient, however exotic, mentioned in this book which cannot be obtained somewhere in this country, even if only in one or two shops. Those who make an occasional marketing trip to Soho or to the region of Tottenham Court Road can buy Greek cheese and Calamata olives, Tahina paste from the Middle East, little birds preserved in olive oil from Cyprus, stuffed vine leaves from Turkey, Spanish sausages, Egyptian brown beans, chick peas, Armenian ham, Spanish, Italian and Cypriot olive oil, Italian salame and rice, even occasionally Neapolitan Mozzarella cheese and honey from Mount Hymettus. These are the details which complete the flavour of a Mediterranean meal, but the ingredients which make this cookery so essentially different from our own are available to all; they are the olive oil, wine, lemons, garlic, onions, tomatoes, and the aromatic herbs and spices which go to make up what is so often lacking in English cooking: variety of flavour and colour, and the warm, rich, stimulating smells of genuine food.

London 1955

24 April

To the Immortal Memory of the Halibut on Which I Dined This Day

Sent with a letter to Unwin, April 26, 1784

William Cowper (1731–1800)

Where hast thou floated, in what seas pursued
Thy pastime? When wast thou an egg new-spawn'd,
Lost in th'immensity of ocean's waste?
Roar as they might, the overbearing winds
That rock'd the deep, thy cradle, thou wast safe –
And in thy minikin and embryo state,
Attach'd to the firm leaf of some salt weed,
Didst outlive tempests, such as wrung and rack'd
The joints of many a stout and gallant bark,
And whelm'd them in the unexplor'd abyss.
Indebted to no magnet and no chart,
Nor under guidance of the polar fire,
Thou wast a voyager on many coasts,
Grazing at large in meadows submarine,
Where flat Batavia just emerging peeps
Above the brine, – where Caledonia's rocks
Beat back the surge, – and where Hibernia shoots
Her wondrous causeway far into the main.
– Wherever thou hast fed, thou little thought'st,
And I not more, that I should feed on thee.
Peace, therefore, and good health, and much good fish,
To him who sent thee! and success, as oft
As it descends into the billowy gulph,
To the same drag that caught thee! – Fare thee well!
Thy lot thy brethren of the slimy fin
Would envy, could they know that thou wast doom'd
To feed a bard, and to be prais'd in verse.

Green Cheese

From *The Appetite of Earth, 1910* | G. K. Chesterton (1874–1936)

Somebody staring into the sky with the same ethereal appetite
declared that the moon was made of green cheese. I never could
conscientiously accept the full doctrine. I am Modernist in this
matter. That the moon is made of cheese I have believed from
childhood; and in the course of every month a giant (of my
acquaintance) bites a big round piece out of it. This seems to me a
doctrine that is above reason, but not contrary to it. But that the
cheese is green seems to be in some degree actually contradicted by
the senses and the reason; first because if the moon were made of
green cheese it would be inhabited; and second because if it were
made of green cheese it would be green. A blue moon is said to be
an unusual sight; but I cannot think that a green one is much more
common. In fact, I think I have seen the moon looking like every
other sort of cheese except a green cheese. I have seen it look exactly
like a cream cheese: a circle of warm white upon a warm faint violet
sky above a cornfield in Kent. I have seen it look very like a Dutch
cheese, rising a dull red copper disk amid masts and dark waters at
Honfleur. I have seen it look like an ordinary sensible Cheddar cheese
in an ordinary sensible Prussian blue sky; and I have once seen it so
naked and ruinous-looking, so strangely lit up, that it looked like a
Gruyère cheese, that awful volcanic cheese that has horrible holes in
it, as if it had come in boiling unnatural milk from mysterious and
unearthly cattle. But I have never yet seen the lunar cheese green;
and I incline to the opinion that the moon is not old enough. The
moon, like everything else, will ripen by the end of the world; and in
the last days we shall see it taking on those volcanic sunset colours,
and leaping with that enormous and fantastic life.

Toasted Cheese

From *Treasure Island, 1883* | Robert Louis Stevenson (1850–1894)

I could now see that he was a white man like myself and that his features were even pleasing. His skin, wherever it was exposed, was burnt by the sun; even his lips were black, and his fair eyes looked quite startling in so dark a face. Of all the beggar-men that I had seen or fancied, he was the chief for raggedness. He was clothed with tatters of old ship's canvas and old sea-cloth, and this extraordinary patchwork was all held together by a system of the most various and incongruous fastenings, brass buttons, bits of stick, and loops of tarry gaskin. About his waist he wore an old brass-buckled leather belt, which was the one thing solid in his whole accoutrement.

'Three years!' I cried. 'Were you shipwrecked?'

'Nay, mate,' said he – 'marooned.'

I had heard the word, and I knew it stood for a horrible kind of punishment common enough among the buccaneers, in which the offender is put ashore with a little powder and shot and left behind on some desolate and distant island.

'Marooned three years agone,' he continued, 'and lived on goats since then, and berries, and oysters. Wherever a man is, says I, a man can do for himself. But, mate, my heart is sore for Christian diet. You mightn't happen to have a piece of cheese about you, now? No? Well, many's the long night I've dreamed of cheese – toasted, mostly – and woke up again, and here I were.'

'If ever I can get aboard again,' said I, 'you shall have cheese by the stone.'

Love

From *Barchester Towers, 1857* | Anthony Trollope (1815–1882)

Madame Neroni:

Don't let love interfere with your appetite. It never does with mine.
Give me half a glass more champagne and then go to the table.

Beefsteak / Beef-Steak ou Bifteck à l'anglaise

From *Le Grand Dictionnaire de la Cuisine, 1873*

Alexandre Dumas (1802–1870)

Translated by Alan (1924–2003) and Jane (1927–2010) Davidson, 1978

I remember seeing the birth of beefsteak in France, after the 1815 campaign, when the English stayed in Paris for two or three years. Until then our cuisine and theirs had been just as separate as our points of view. It was therefore not without a certain trepidation that one saw beefsteak trying to introduce itself slyly into our kitchens. Yet, we are an eclectic people and without prejudice. So, as soon as we had realized that, in spite of 'coming from the Greeks, it was not poisoned,' before we held out our plates, and gave beefsteak its citizenship papers.

Beefsteak and More

From *A Tramp Abroad, 1880* | Mark Twain (1835–1910)

They have it in Europe, but they don't know how to cook it. Neither will they cut it right. It comes on the table in a small, round pewter platter. It lies in the center of this platter, in a bordering bed of grease-soaked potatoes; it is the size, shape, and thickness of a man's hand with the thumb and fingers cut off. It is a little overdone, is rather dry, it tastes pretty insipidly, it rouses no enthusiasm.

Imagine a poor exile contemplating that inert thing; and imagine an angel suddenly sweeping down out of a better land and setting before him a mighty porter-house steak an inch and a half thick, hot and sputtering from the griddle; dusted with a fragrant pepper; enriched with little melting bits of butter of the most unimpeachable freshness and genuineness; the precious juices of the meat trickling out and joining the gravy, archipelagoed with mushrooms; a township or two of tender, yellowish fat gracing an outlying district of this ample county of beefsteak; the long white bone which divides the sirloin from the tenderloin still in its place; and imagine that the angel also adds a great cup of American home-made coffee, with a cream a-froth on top, some real butter, firm and yellow and fresh, some smoking hot biscuits, a plate of hot buckwheat cakes, with transparent syrup – could words describe the gratitude of this exile?

MAY

Between Luxury and Abstinence

Markets and Travellers

From *Family Life, 1996* | Elisabeth Luard (1942–)

Andalusia:

If a nation's character and history is to be read in the market-place, Algeciras remained staunchly Moorish in its gastronomic tastes. The gathering of country and town, merchants and sailors, has always provided a forum for the exchange of ideas – so perhaps it is not surprising that the market-snack is the first culinary bridgehead to be captured as a result of immigration, or colonial involvement, or simply in response to the tastes of migrant workers.

In the spice-merchant's sacks could be seen the evidence of the ancient trade routes, traces of conquest, the indelible evidence of colonial adventuring. It was Phoenician traders who first brought the saffron which perfumes the rice dishes of Andalusia, the powdery scents of cumin and turmeric, cloves and cinnamon spoke of the centuries of Moorish occupation; precious phials of vanilla pods told us of the long Atlantic voyage to discover the New World. Golden oil and pale straw wines of Jerez, the product of olive groves and vines planted by the Romans, were evidence of that earlier colonization. Roman wine provided yeast to leaven Andalusian bread. Two thousand years later, nowhere can the legacy of Rome be more clearly seen than in the daily dinner.

1 May

Whimsical Drinks

From *Lothair, 1870* | Benjamin Disraeli (1804–1881)

The sun had set in glory over the broad expanse of waters still
glowing in the dying beam; the people were assembled in thousands
on the borders of the lake, in the centre of which was an island with
a pavilion. Fanciful barges and gondolas of various shapes and
colours were waiting for Lothair and his party, to carry them over
to the pavilion, where they found a repast which became the hour
and the scene: coffee and ices and whimsical drinks, which sultanas
would sip in Arabian tales.

A Dinner with Philosophers and Learned Men

From *Letters from a Citizen of the World to his Friends in the East, 1760–1761* | Oliver Goldsmith (1728–1774)

Letter LVII

From Lien Chi Altangi to Fum Hoam, first President of the Ceremonial Academy at Pekin in China.

I expected an entertainment where we should have much reasoning and little meet.

. . . .

3 May

The appearance of dinner, which consisted of a variety of dishes, seemed to diffuse a new cheerfulness upon every face; so that I now expected the philosophical conversation to begin, as they improved in good humour. The principal priest, however, opened his mouth with only observing, that the venison had not been kept long enough, though he gave strict orders for having it killed ten days before. 'I fear,' continued he, 'it will be found to want the true healthy flavour; you will find nothing of the original wildness in it.' A priest, who sat next to him, having smelt it, and wiped his nose, 'Ah, my good lord,' cries he, 'you are too modest, it is perfectly fine; every body knows that nobody understands keeping; venison with your lordship.' – 'Ay, and partridges too,' interrupted another; 'I never find them right any where else.'

A Man of Taste

From *Crotchet Castle, 1831* | Thomas Love Peacock (1785–1866)

The Rev. Dr. Folliott:

You are a man of taste, Mr. Crotchet. A man of taste is seen at once in the array of his breakfast-table.

. . . .

Chocolate, coffee, tea, cream, eggs, ham, tongue, cold fowl, all these are good, and bespeak good knowledge in him who sets them forth: but the touchstone is fish: anchovy is the first step, prawns and shrimps the second; and I laud him who reaches even to these: potted char and lampreys are the third, and a fine stretch of progression; but lobster is, indeed, matter for a May morning, and demands a rare combination of knowledge and virtue in him who sets it forth.

4 May

The Hony-combe

Robert Herrick (1591–1674)

If thou hast found an honie-combe,
Eate thou not all, but taste on some:
For if thou eat'st it to excess;
That sweetness turnes to Loathsomness.
Taste it to Temper; then 'twill be
Marrow, and Manna unto thee.

Storing Honey

From *The Country Housewife's Garden, 1617*

William Lawson (c. 1554–1635)

Usual vessels are of clay, but after wood be satiated with honey
(for it will leak at first: for honey is marvellously searching, though
thick, and therefore virtuous) I use it rather because it will not break
so soon, with falls, frosts, or otherwise, and greater Vessels of clay
will hardly last.

When you use your Honey, with a spoon take off the skin, which it
hath put up.

6 May

Some Notes About Honey

From *The Closet of the Eminently Learned Sir Kenelme Digbie Kt. Opened, 1669* | Sir Kenelm Digby (1603–1665)

The Honey of dry open Countries, where there is much Wild-thyme, Rosemary, and Flowers, is best. It is of three sorts, Virgin-honey, Life-honey, and Stock-honey. The first is the best. The Life-honey next. The Virgin-honey is of Bees, that swarmed the Spring before, and are taken up in Autumn; and is made best by chusing the Whitest combs of the Hive, and then letting the Honey run out of them lying upon a Sieve without pressing it, or breaking of the Combs. The Life-honey is of the same Combs broken after the Virgin-honey is run from it; The Merchants of Honey do use to mingle all the sorts together. The first of a swarm is called Virgin-honey. That of the next year, after the Swarm was hatched, is Life-honey. And ever after, it is Honey of Old-stocks. Honey that is forced out of the Combs, will always taste of Wax. Hampshire Honey is most esteemed at London. About Bisleter there is excellent good. Some account Norfolk honey the best.

The Festival of Afternoon Tea

From *The Private Papers of Henry Ryecroft, 1903*

George Gissing (1857–1903)

In nothing is the English genius for domesticity more notably
declared than in the institution of this festival – almost one may call
it so – of afternoon tea. Beneath simple roofs, the hour of tea has
something in it of sacred; for it marks the end of domestic work and
worry, the beginning of restful, sociable evening. The mere chink of
cups and saucers tunes the mind to happy repose. I care nothing for
your five o'clock tea of modish drawing-rooms, idle and wearisome
like all else in which that world has part; I speak of tea where one
is *at home* in quite another than the worldly sense. To admit mere
strangers to your tea-table is profanation; on the other hand, English
hospitality has here its kindliest aspect; never is friend more welcome
than when he drops in for a cup of tea. Where tea is really a meal,
with nothing between it and nine o'clock supper, it is – again in the
true sense – the *homeliest* meal of the day. Is it believable that the
Chinese, in who knows how many centuries, have derived from tea
a millionth part of the pleasure or the good which it has brought to
England in the past one hundred years?

Crumbly Cake

From *Framley Parsonage: Mrs Proudie's Conversazione, 1861*

Anthony Trollope (1815–1882)

Four times during the two hours' period of her conversazione tea and cake were to be handed round on salvers. It is astonishing how far a very little cake will go in this way, particularly if administered tolerably early after dinner. The men can't eat it, and the women, having no plates and no table, are obliged to abstain. Mrs. Jones knows that she cannot hold a piece of crumbly cake in her hand till it be consumed without doing serious injury to her best dress.

9 May

Coffee

From *The Diary, 1637* | John Evelyn (1620–1706)

Edited by William Bray (1736–1832)

10th May

There came in my time to the College [Balliol] one Nathaniel
Conopios, out of Greece, from Cyrill, the patriarch of
Constantinople, who, returning many years after, was made (as I
understand) Bishop of Smyrna. He was the first I ever saw drink
coffee; which custom came not into England till thirty years after.*

*Evelyn should have said 'till twenty years after,' not thirty. Coffee
was introduced into England, and coffee-houses set up, in 1658.
(William Bray)

A Packed Lunch

From *A Girl of the Limberlost, 1909* | Gene Stratton-Porter (1863–1924)

Mrs. Comstock was up early, and without a word handed Elnora the case as she left the next morning.

'Thank you, mother,' said Elnora, and went on her way.

She walked down the road looking straight ahead until she came to the corner, where she usually entered the swamp. She paused, glanced that way and smiled. Then she turned and looked back. There was no one coming in any direction. She followed the road until well around the corner, then she stopped and sat on a grassy spot, laid her books beside her and opened the lunch-box. Last night's odours had in a measure prepared her for what she would see, but not quite. She scarcely could believe her senses. Half the bread compartment was filled with dainty sandwiches of bread and butter sprinkled with the yolk of egg and the remainder with three large slices of the most fragrant spice cake imaginable. The meat dish contained shaved cold ham, of which she knew the quality, the salad was tomatoes and celery, and the cup held preserved pear, clear as amber. There was milk in the bottle, two tissue-wrapped cucumber pickles in the folding drinking-cup, and a fresh napkin in the ring. No lunch was ever daintier or more palatable; of that Elnora was perfectly sure. And her mother had prepared it for her!

Microwave Ovens

From *The Bachelor Home Companion, 1987*

P. J. O'Rourke (1947–2022)

Best used as toys:

Crumple up aluminium foil and watch it sparkle there. See what microwaves do to a sealed can of creamed corn. Find out if the thing will dry slush-soaked dress shoes. (So much for the $200 Bally tassel loafers.) But for actual cooking you'll find food that comes out of a microwave is every bit as bad as food that comes out of a regular oven, just quicker. Therefore you're not as hungry. So the food tastes even worse than it was going to, and that was bad enough. Also microwaves don't give you time to have five or six flavour-deadening drinks while the Swanson Hungry-Man Salisbury Steak Dinner is getting black around the edges.

Fixed Principles

From *The Tenant of Wildfell Hall, 1848* | Anne Brontë (1820–1849)

[The Reverend Michael Millward] was a man of fixed principles, strong prejudices, and regular habits – intolerant of dissent in any shape, acting under a firm conviction that *his* opinions were always right, and whoever differed from them, must be, either most deplorably ignorant, or wilfully blind.

. . . .

He had a laudable care for his own bodily health – kept very early hours, regularly took a walk before breakfast, was vastly particular about warm and dry clothing, had never been known to preach a sermon without previously swallowing a raw egg – albeit he was gifted with good lungs and a powerful voice, – and was, generally, extremely particular about what he ate and drank, though by no means abstemious, and having a mode of dietary peculiar to himself, – being a great despiser of tea and such slops, and a patron of malt liquors, bacon and eggs, ham, hung beef, and other strong meats, which agreed well enough with his digestive organs, and therefore were maintained by him to be good and wholesome for everybody, and confidently recommended to the most delicate convalescents or dyspeptics, who, if they failed to derive the promised benefit from his prescriptions, were told it was because they had not persevered, and if they complained of inconvenient results therefrom, were assured it was all fancy.

13 May

Appetite and Digestion

From *Macbeth, 1606*, Act III, Scene iv | William Shakespeare (1564–1616)

Macbeth:

Now, good digestion wait on appetite,

And health on both!

Read, Mark, Learn
and Inwardly Digest

From *Feeding the Mind, 1907* | Lewis Carroll (1832–1898)

The consequences of neglecting the body can be clearly seen and felt; and it might be well for some if the mind were equally visible and tangible – if we could take it, say, to the doctor, and have its pulse felt.

'Why, what have you been doing with this mind lately? How have you fed it? It looks pale, and the pulse is very slow.'

'Well, doctor, it has not had much regular food lately. I gave it a lot of sugar-plums yesterday.'

'Sugar-plums! What kind?'

'Well, they were a parcel of conundrums, sir.'

'Ah, I thought so. Now just mind this: if you go on playing tricks like that, you'll spoil all its teeth, and get laid up with mental indigestion. You must have nothing but the plainest reading for the next few days. Take care now! No novels on any account!'

Aunt Chloe

From *Uncle Tom's Cabin, 1852* | Harriet Beecher Stowe (1811–1896)

A cook she certainly was, in the very bone and centre of her soul.
Her corn-cake, in all its varieties of hoe-cake, dodgers, muffins, and
other species too numerous to mention, was a sublime mystery to all
less practised compounders; and she would shake her fat sides with
honest pride and merriment, as she would narrate the fruitless
efforts that one and another of her compeers had made to attain to
her elevation.

16 May

They Who Prepare My Evening Meal Below

Henry David Thoreau (1817–1862)

They who prepare my evening meal below
Carelessly hit the kettle as they go
With tongs or shovel,
And ringing round and round,
Out of this hovel
It makes an eastern temple by the sound.

At first I thought a cow bell right at hand
Mid birches sounded o'er the open land,
Where I plucked flowers
Many years ago,
Spending midsummer hours
With such secure delight they hardly seemed to flow.

American Cooking

From *Domestic Manners of the Americans, 1832*

Fanny Trollope (1779–1863)

In relating all I know of America, I surely must not omit so
important a feature as the cooking. There are sundry anomalies in
the mode of serving even a first-rate table; but as these are altogether
matters of custom, they by no means indicate either indifference or
neglect in this important business; and whether castors are placed on
the table or on the sideboard; whether soup, fish, patties, and salad
be eaten in orthodox order or not, signifies but little. I am hardly
capable, I fear, of giving a very erudite critique on the subject; general
observations therefore must suffice. The ordinary mode of living is
abundant, but not delicate. They consume an extraordinary quantity
of bacon. Ham and beef-steaks appear morning, noon, and night.
In eating, they mix things together with the strangest incongruity
imaginable. I have seen eggs and oysters eaten together: the
sempiternal ham with apple-sauce; beefsteak with stewed peaches;
and salt fish with onions. The bread is everywhere excellent, but they
rarely enjoy it themselves, as they insist upon eating horrible half-
baked hot rolls both morning and evening. The butter is tolerable;
but they have seldom such cream as every little dairy produces in
England; in fact, the cows are very roughly kept, compared with
our's. Common vegetables are abundant and very fine. I never saw
sea-cale or cauliflowers, and either from the want of summer rain, or
the want of care, the harvest of green vegetables is much sooner over
than with us. They eat the Indian corn in a great variety of forms;
sometimes it is dressed green, and eaten like peas; sometimes it is
broken to pieces when dry, boiled plain, and brought to table like
rice; this dish is called hominy. The flour of it is made into at least a
dozen different sorts of cakes; but in my opinion all bad. This flour,
mixed in the proportion of one-third with fine wheat, makes by far
the best bread I ever tasted.

Golden Rules for the Kitchen

From *The Book of Household Management, 1861*

Mrs Isabella Beeton (1836–1865)

Without *cleanliness* and *punctuality* good Cooking is *impossible*.

Leave nothing *dirty*; *clean and clear as you go*.

A time for everything and *everything in time*.

A good Cook *wastes nothing*.

An hour lost *in the morning* has to be run after *all day*.

Haste *without hurry* saves worry, fuss and flurry.

Stew *boiled* is Stew *spoiled*.

Strong fire for *Roasting*; *clear* fire for *Broiling*.

Wash Vegetables in *three* waters.

Boil fish *quickly*, meat *slowly*.

19 May

Salad

From *The Physiology of Taste, 1825*

Jean Anthelme Brillat-Savarin (1755–1826)

Translated by Fayette Robinson, 1854

Dinner with the Curé:

The table was very well arranged; Old wine sparkled in a crystal flagon, and the porcelain was faultless. The plates were kept hot by boiling water, and an old housekeeper was in attendance.

The meal was half way between luxury and abstinence. A soup of écrevisses was removed and a salmon trout, an omelette, and a salad were placed on the table.

'My dinner tells you,' said the priest 'what you do not know, that to day is a fast day.'

. . . .

Then came the salad. (I recommend it to those who have confidence in me. It refreshes without exciting. I think it makes people younger.)

Shoebox Lunches

From *Black Food, 2021* | Bryant Terry (1974–)

Twentieth-century African American travel culture was profoundly
shaped by the historical oppression of Black communities'
rights to free movement. From the 1890s until 1965, Jim Crow
segregation laws legitimized the isolation of public spaces, schools,
transportation, restrooms, and restaurants exclusively for white
people. 'The vast majority of the country was composed of white
spaces where black people were forbidden or unwelcome,'
Dr. Gretchen Sorin wrote in her article, *The Negro Travelers Green
Book*. For the Black traveler, accessing food along journeys was nearly
impossible. In response, Black women would arm Black travelers
with 'shoebox lunches'.

At times faceless and unsung, these women – family members,
church attendees, or businesswomen – would find ways, both
legal and illegal (as hawkers) to cook delicious meals with limited
resources, making a way out of no way.

Patience

From *Ammu, 2022* | Asma Khan (1969–)

The most precious ingredient you are putting into a dish is your time. You can buy all the ingredients again, but that moment you spent cooking is a precious gift to those who will share that meal with you. Ammu would always tell me that the greatest attributes of a good cook are generosity and patience. Generosity not in buying expensive ingredients but in cooking with your heart. Patience is something that is never emphasised enough when it comes to cooking. This is not to be confused with a long, hard slog. Patience is waiting for things to marinate, for the dough to rest, to gently wash the rice … just giving each step the time it needs.

22 May

Time to Make a Garden

From *Death Comes for the Archbishop, 1927*

Willa Cather (1873–1947)

On coming into the dining-room, Bishop Latour placed his candlesticks over the fire-place, since there were already six upon the table, illuminating the brown soup-pot. After they had stood for a moment in prayer, Father Joseph lifted the cover and ladled the soup into the plates, a dark onion soup with croutons. The Bishop tasted it critically and smiled at his companion. After the spoon had travelled to his lips a few times, he put it down and leaning back in his chair remarked,

'Think of it, *Blanchet*; in all this vast country between the Mississippi and the Pacific Ocean, there is probably not another human being who could make a soup like this.'

'Not unless he is a Frenchman.' said Father Joseph. He had tucked a napkin over the front of his cassock and was losing no time in reflection.

'I am not deprecating your individual talent, Joseph,' the Bishop continued, 'but, when one thinks of it, a soup like this is not the work of one man. It is the result of a constantly refined tradition. There are nearly a thousand years of history in this soup.'

Father Joseph frowned intently at the earthen pot in the middle of the table. His pale, near-sighted eyes had always the look of peering into distance. '*C'est ça, c'est vrai,*' he murmured. 'But how,' he exclaimed as he filled the Bishop's plate again, 'how can a man make a proper soup without leeks, that king of vegetables? We cannot go on eating onions for ever.'

After carrying away the *soupière*, he brought in the roast chicken and *pommes sautées*. 'And salad, Jean,' he continued as he began to carve. 'Are we to eat dried beans and roots for the rest of our lives? Surely we must find time to make a garden.'

The Practicalities

From *Cooking in Ten Minutes / La Cuisine en dix minutes, ou l'Adaptation au rythme moderne*, 1930 |

Édouard de Pomiane (1875–1964)

Translated by Peggie Benton

The moment you come into the kitchen light the gas. Ten-minute cookery is impossible without gas.

Put a large saucepan of water onto the fire. Slip on the lid and let it boil.

What is the use of this water, you will ask? I don't know. But it is bound to be useful, either for cooking or washing up or making coffee.

If you are going to fry something don't wait to take off your hat before putting the pan on the fire. The time during which the fat melts and reaches the proper temperature does not count in the preparation of our meal.

The fire is busy. Now turn your attention to the cooking.

There are four different ways of using heat for cooking: 1. Boiling, or cooking in water. 2. Cooking in fat or frying. 3. Cooking on an open flame (grilling). 4. Steaming.

In our case, that is to say when time is short, steaming is almost out of the question. It is a long, slow business and best avoided by people in a hurry.

We will keep to the first three ways of cooking.

Tradition

From *Honey from a Weed, 1986* | Patience Gray (1917–2005)

In my experience it is the countryman who is the real gourmet and for good reason; it is he who has cultivated, raised, hunted or fished the raw materials and has made the wine himself. The preoccupation of his wife to do justice to his labours and bring the outcome triumphantly to table. In this an emotional element is involved. Perhaps this very old approach is beginning once again to inspire those who cook in more complex urban situations.

In my view it was not necessarily the chefs of prelates and princes who invented dishes. Country people and fishermen created them, great chefs refined them and wrote them down. In Latin countries, because of inborn conservatism, the tradition is alive and we can learn from it, that is, learning from people who have never read a book.

Forbidden Fruit

Emily Dickinson (1830–1886)

Forbidden Fruit a flavor has
That lawful Orchards mocks –
How luscious lies within the Pod
The Pea that Duty locks –

Culinary Links

From *Good Things in England, 1932* | Florence White (1863–1940)

Our kitchen has more in common with America than with any other country. This is natural, as the foundations of both the English and American kitchens were the same up to 1620; England is proud of the national kitchen American women have developed on their own individual lines, and one of the great interests of this, the *direct* research, collated with the writings of authorities on which the present book is based, has been to come across continual evidence of our common family interests with our cousins across the Atlantic.

In a new and vast country far from Europe they have been able to preserve the integrity of their own kitchen far better than we have, and to develop it on individual lines. If we want to learn how to improve our own cookery – and we should want to do this – it is to America we should turn to, not to France. French cookery is of course very good, but there has always been a great sameness about it; its chief merit lies in its fixed, unchanging system; every French cook is splendidly trained on exactly the same lines, and can therefore serve in any kitchen controlled by a French chef. This also helps France to preserve the individuality of its own cuisine and advertise it as they have done with so much success. But it cannot be allowed to crush out our individual English kitchen or even to take credit for its many merits. The Scots kitchen owes more to France than does our English kitchen.

We can learn from the Commonwealth countries. They have the same advantage as America of developing the cookery of the Homeland in a new setting. We have much in common also with Norway, Sweden, Denmark and Holland. According to a leader in *The Times* (December 12 1931), 'It is a common saying that a man is what he eats, and equally common that character is destiny, so that it seems logical that if we eat what our forefathers ate, we shall become like them and enjoy some of their good fortune.' And we have Viking blood in our veins.

Baking and Cookerie

From *Five Hundred Points of Good Husbandry, 1557, 1573*

Thomas Tusser (c. 1524–1580)

Baking

Newe bread is a drivell.

Much crust is as evill.

1. New bread is a waster, but mouldie is wurse.
    what that way dog catcheth, that loseth the purse.

2. Much dowebake I praise not, much crust is as ill,
    the meane is the Huswife, say nay if ye will.

Cookerie

Good cookerie craveth.

Good turnebroch saveth.

1. Good cooke to dresse dinner, to bake and to brewe,
    deserves a rewarde, being honest and trewe.
2. Good diligent turnebroch and trustie withall,
    is sometime as needfull as some in the hall.

Subtle Insults

From *The Autobiography of Alice B. Toklas, 1933*

Gertrude Stein (1874–1946)

Hélène had her opinions, she did not for instance like Matisse. She said a frenchman should not stay unexpectedly to a meal particularly if he asked the servant beforehand what there was for dinner. She said foreigners had a perfect right to do these things but not a frenchman and Matisse had once done it. So when Miss Stein said to her, Monsieur Matisse is staying for dinner this evening, she would say, in that case I will not make an omelette but fry the eggs. It takes the same number of eggs and the same amount of butter but it shows less respect, and he will understand.

29 May

The Snack

From *In Defence of Food, 2008* | Michael Pollan (1955–)

The biggest threat to the meal-as-we-knew-it is surely the snack, and snacking in recent years has colonized whole new parts of our day and places in our lives. Work, for example, used to be a more or less food-free stretch of time between meals, but no longer. Offices now typically have well-stocked kitchens, and it is apparently considered gauche at a business meeting or conference if a spread of bagels, muffins, pastries and soft drinks is not provided at frequent intervals. Attending a recent conference on nutrition and health, of all things, I was astounded to see that in addition to the copious buffet at breakfast, lunch and dinner, our hosts wheeled out a copious buffet between breakfast and lunch and then again halfway between lunch and dinner, evidently worried that we would not be able to survive the long crossing from one meal to the next without a between-meal meal.

I may be showing my age, but didn't there used to be at least a mild social taboo against the between-meal snack?

The Song Against Grocers

G. K. Chesterton (1874–1936)

God made the wicked Grocer
For a mystery and a sign,
That men might shun the awful shops
And go to inns to dine;
Where the bacon's on the rafter
And the wine is in the wood,
And God that made good laughter
Has seen that they are good.

The evil-hearted Grocer
Would call his mother 'Ma'am,'
And bow at her and bob at her,
Her aged soul to damn,
And rub his horrid hands and ask
What article was next
Though *mortis in articulo*
Should be her proper text.

His props are not his children,
But pert lads underpaid,
Who call out 'Cash!' and bang about
To work his wicked trade;
He keeps a lady in a cage
Most cruelly all day,
And makes her count and calls her 'Miss'
Until she fades away.

The righteous minds of innkeepers
Induce them now and then
To crack a bottle with a friend
Or treat unmoneyed men,

But who hath seen the Grocer
Treat housemaids to his teas
Or crack a bottle of fish sauce
Or stand a man a cheese?

He sells us sands of Araby
As sugar for cash down;
He sweeps his shop and sells the dust
The purest salt in town,
He crams with cans of poisoned meat
Poor subjects of the King,
And when they die by thousands
Why, he laughs like anything.

The wicked Grocer groces
In spirits and in wine,
Not frankly and in fellowship
As men in inns do dine;
But packed with soap and sardines
And carried off by grooms,
For to be snatched by Duchesses
And drunk in dressing-rooms.

The hell-instructed Grocer
Has a temple made of tin,
And the ruin of good innkeepers
Is loudly urged therein;
But now the sands are running out
From sugar of a sort,
The Grocer trembles; for his time,
Just like his weight, is short.

JUNE

An Air of Profusion

Salad

From *Simple French Cooking for English Homes, 1923*

Xavier Marcel Boulestin (1878–1943)

One cannot help wondering if an English salad is the result of ignorance or the aim of a curiously perverted taste.

A salad must be fresh and crisp, its flavour sharp and appetizing. The ingredients with which it is made all have these qualities; so has the seasoning. Indeed, to make it sickly amounts to a *tour de force* which must be very difficult to accomplish. Still, most English cooks seem to be very successful in their attempt with the help of cream sauces, sham *mayonnaises* and the addition of the fatal radish, the strong taste of which absolutely kills that of the other vegetables.

Rumour has it that, somewhere in America, they can make salads, although of a complicated kind and queer flavour; and I am assured by travelers that they taste more like strong cocktails than refreshing vegetable dishes.

I must give France its due. The French, I am told, have many failings, but they can make wine, coffee and salads.

Recipe for a Salad

Rev. Sydney Smith (1771–1845)

To make this condiment your poet begs
The pounded yellow of two hard-boil'd eggs;
Two boil'd potatoes, pass'd through kitchen sieve,
Smoothness and softness to the salad give.
Let onion atoms lurk within the bowl,
And, half suspected, animate the whole.
Of mordant mustard add a single spoon,
Distrust the condiment that bites so soon;
But deem it not, thou man of herbs, a fault,
To add a double quantity of salt;
Four times the spoon with oil from Lucca brown,
And twice with vinegar, procured from town;
And lastly, o'er the flavoured compound toss
A magic soupçon of anchovy sauce.
Oh, green and glorious! Oh, herbaceous treat!
'Twould tempt the dying anchorite to eat:
Back to the world he'd turn his fleeting soul,
And plunge his fingers in the salad-bowl;
Serenely full, the epicure would say,
Fate cannot harm me, I have dined to-day.

Hold the Mayo

From *Feast Days, 1990* | Jennifer Paterson (1928–1999)

The Spectator, 1986

There are a lot of very terrible food advertisements that appear regularly on our television screens with ghastly plates of something with neat piles of bright cylindrical carrots and emerald peas stuck to attention, but the worst ones are for the yellowish goo they pour out of bottles to desecrate salads and tomatoes. There is usually some poor old egg brought into the action. Why in all the world do the British like this vile-tasting stuff called salad cream or even worse mayonnaise? It has nothing to do with either, more like a mixture of malt vinegar and Scotts Emulsion. I have even had it served with an otherwise excellent salmon in an otherwise perfectly respectable country hotel in Cumberland.

Then there is the terrible question of trying to get a plain, well-dressed salad, almost impossible; along comes a limp lettuce with beetroot bleeding all over it, liberally laced with malt vinegar and strewn with the ubiquitous mustard and cress we used to grow on flannels, and some chunks of tomato thrown in for good measure – disastrous mess. Salads should remain simple and green when lettuce is used.

Eating Too Much

From *The Tale of Peter Rabbit, privately printed 1901,
published 1902* | Beatrix Potter (1866–1943)

Flopsy, Mopsy, and Cotton-tail, who were good little bunnies, went
down the lane to gather blackberries;

But Peter, who was very naughty, ran straight away to Mr.
McGregor's garden, and squeezed under the gate!

First he ate some lettuces and some French beans; and then he ate
some radishes;

And then, feeling rather sick, he went to look for some parsley.

4 June

189

Going Without Dinner

From *The Importance of Being Earnest, 1895*

Oscar Wilde (1854–1900)

ALGERNON.

You can't possibly ask me to go without having some dinner. It's absurd. I never go without my dinner. No one ever does, except vegetarians and people like that.

Vegetarian Restaurants

From *The Private Papers of Henry Ryecroft, 1903*

George Gissing (1857–1903)

There is to me an odd pathos in the literature of vegetarianism.
I remember the day when I read these periodicals and pamphlets
with all the zest of hunger and poverty, vigorously seeking to
persuade myself that flesh was an altogether superfluous, and even a
repulsive, food. If ever such things fall under my eyes nowadays,
I am touched with a half humorous compassion for the people whose
necessity, not their will, consents to this chemical view of diet. There
comes before me a vision of certain vegetarian restaurants, where,
at a minimal outlay, I have often enough made believe to satisfy my
craving stomach; where I have swallowed 'savoury cutlet,' 'vegetable
steak,' and I know not what windy insufficiencies tricked up under
specious names. One place do I recall where you had a complete
dinner for sixpence – I dare not try to remember the items. But well
indeed do I see the faces of the guests – poor clerks and shopboys,
bloodless girls and women of many sorts – all endeavouring to
find a relish in lentil soup and haricot something-or-other. It was a
grotesquely heart-breaking sight.

Arctic Roll

From *Toast*, 2003 | Nigel Slater (1956–)

There were only three of us at school whose house wasn't joined to the one next door. Number 67 Sandringham Road, always referred to as 'York House', had mock-Tudor wooden beams, a double garage of which one half doubled as a garden shed and repository for my brothers' canoes, and a large crumbling greenhouse. I was also the only one ever to have tasted Arctic Roll. While my friends made do with the pink, white and brown stripes of a Neapolitan ice-cream brick, my father would bring out this newfangled frozen gourmet dessert. Arctic Roll was a sponge-covered tube of vanilla ice-cream, its USP being the wrapping of wet sponge and ring of red jam so thin it could have been drawn on with an architect's pen.

In Wolverhampton, Arctic Roll was considered to be something of a status symbol. It contained mysteries, too. Why, for instance, does the ice cream not melt when the sponge defrosts? How is it possible to spread the jam that thin? How come it was made from sponge cake, jam and ice cream yet managed to taste of cold cardboard? And most importantly, how come cold cardboard tasted so good?

As treats go, this was the big one, bigger even than Cadbury's MiniRoll. This wasn't a holiday or celebration treat like trifle. This was a treat for no obvious occasion. Its appearance had nothing to do with being good, having done well in a school test, having been kind or thoughtful. It was just a treat, served with as much pomp as if it were a roasted swan at a Tudor banquet. I think it was a subtle reminder to the assembled family and friends of how well my father's business was going. Whatever, there was no food that received such an ovation in our house. Quite an achievement for something I always thought tasted like a frozen carpet.

London Bread

From *The Expedition of Humphry Clinker, 1771*

Tobias Smollett (1721–1771)

London, June 8

To Dr Lewis

The bread I eat in London, is a deleterious paste, mixed up with chalk, alum, and bone-ashes; insipid to the taste, and destructive to the constitution. The good people are not ignorant of this adulteration – but they prefer it to wholesome bread, because it is whiter than the meal of corn: thus they sacrifice their taste and their health, and the lives of their tender infants, to a most absurd gratification of a mis-judging eye; and the miller, or the baker, is obliged to poison them and their families, in order to live by his profession.

8 June

White Bread

From *How to Cook a Wolf, 1942* | M. F. K. Fisher (1908–1992)

The English Food Ministry has been trying ever since the Second
World War began to make its subjects buy whole-cereal breads rather
than the emasculated pale stuff sold by every self-respecting bakery.
Apparently class snobbism has conquered once more over good
sense, for no matter what proof the Ministry gives that white bread
will cause bad teeth, poor eyes, weak back, fatigue, the Britishers go
on eating what has for decades meant refinement and 'good taste',
socially if not gastronomically.

9 June

My Neighbour's House

From *The Great Gatsby, 1925* | F. Scott Fitzgerald (1896–1940)

There was music from my neighbour's house through the summer nights. In his blue gardens men and girls came and went like moths among the whisperings and the champagne and the stars. At high tide in the afternoon I watched his guests diving from the tower of his raft or taking the sun on the hot sand of his beach while his two motor-boats slit the waters of the Sound, drawing aquaplanes over cataracts of foam. On week-ends his Rolls-Royce became an omnibus, bearing parties to and from the city, between nine in the morning and long past midnight, while his station wagon scampered like a brisk yellow bug to meet all trains. And on Mondays eight servants including an extra gardener toiled all day with mops and scrubbing-brushes and hammers and garden-shears, repairing the ravages of the night before.

Every Friday five crates of oranges and lemons arrived from a fruiterer in New York – every Monday these same oranges and lemons left his back door in a pyramid of pulp-less halves. There was a machine in the kitchen which could extract the juice of two hundred oranges in half an hour, if a little button was pressed two hundred times by a butler's thumb.

At least once a fortnight a corps of caterers came down with several hundred feet of canvas and enough coloured lights to make a Christmas tree of Gatsby's enormous garden. On buffet tables, garnished with glistening hors-d'oeuvre, spiced baked hams crowded against salads of harlequin designs and pastry pigs and turkeys bewitched to a dark gold. In the main hall a bar with a real brass rail was set up, and stocked with gins and liquors and with cordials so long forgotten that most of his female guests were too young to know one from another.

Bertie Bott's Every-Flavour Beans

From *Harry Potter and the Philosopher's Stone, 1997*

J. K. Rowling (1965–)

'You want to be careful with those,' Ron warned Harry. 'When they say every flavour, they mean every flavour – you know, you get all the ordinary ones like chocolate and peppermint and marmalade, but then you can get spinach and liver and tripe. George reckons he had a bogey-flavoured one once.'

Ron picked up a green bean, looked at it carefully and bit into a corner.

'Bleaaargh – see? Sprouts.'

They had a good time eating the Every-Flavour Beans. Harry got toast, coconut, baked bean, strawberry, curry, grass, coffee, sardine and was even brave enough to nibble the end off a funny grey one Ron wouldn't touch, which turned out to be pepper.

11 June

Holliday or Melty Butter?

From *Freud on Food, 1978* | Clement Freud (1924–2009)

Recently in a newish London Club which has members who are still very much better than the food, I ordered asparagus. 'Certainly,' said the highly trained waiter: 'you wante sparagus holliday or melty butter?' I said hollandaise would be nice – and we smiled at each other (there is always that moment of friendship before the first whitebait is flung into your lap). The asparagus arrived, cooked to the point of submission; consequently I was unsurprised to note that the hollandaise sauce had curdled. I could have uncurdled it in my wine glass – which would have been ostentatious, though not difficult: start with a dessertspoonful of cream or dry white wine and teaspoon the well-mixed curdled sauce on to this, whisking with a fork. Or I could have made a scene and embarrassed my host … or have eaten the stuff and done untold harm to my *amour propre*.

Afternoon Tea

From *The Portrait of a Lady, 1881*

Henry James (1843–1916)

Under certain circumstances there are few hours in life more
agreeable than the hour dedicated to the ceremony known as
afternoon tea. There are circumstances in which, whether you
partake of the tea or not – some people of course never do, – the
situation is in itself delightful. Those that I have in mind in
beginning to unfold this simple history offered an admirable setting
to an innocent pastime. The implements of the little feast had been
disposed upon the lawn of an old English country-house, in what
I should call the perfect middle of a splendid summer afternoon. Part
of the afternoon had waned, but much of it was left, and what was
left was of the finest and rarest quality. Real dusk would not arrive
for many hours; but the flood of summer light had begun to ebb,
the air had grown mellow, the shadows were long upon the smooth,
dense turf. They lengthened slowly, however, and the scene expressed
that sense of leisure still to come which is perhaps the chief source of
one's enjoyment of such a scene at such an hour. From five o'clock to
eight is on certain occasions a little eternity; but on such an occasion
as this the interval could be only an eternity of pleasure.

Suggestions

From *Alice's Adventures in Wonderland*, 1865

Lewis Carroll (1832–1898)

The table was a large one, but the three were all crowded together at one corner of it. 'No room! No room!' they cried out when they saw Alice coming. 'There's *plenty* of room!' said Alice indignantly, and she sat down in a large arm-chair at one end of the table.

'Have some wine,' the March Hare said in an encouraging tone.

Alice looked all round the table, but there was nothing on it but tea. 'I don't see any wine,' she remarked.

'There isn't any,' said the March Hare.

'Then it wasn't very civil of you to offer it,' said Alice angrily.

'It wasn't very civil of you to sit down without being invited,' said the March Hare.

'I didn't know it was *your* table,' said Alice: 'it's laid for a great many more than three.'

. . . .

'It's always six o'clock now.' [said the Hatter]

A bright idea came into Alice's head. 'Is that the reason so many tea-things are put out here?' she asked.

'Yes, that's it,' said the Hatter with a sigh: 'it's always tea-time, and we've no time to wash the things between whiles.'

'Then you keep moving round, I suppose?' said Alice.

'Exactly so,' said the Hatter: 'as the things get used up.'

'But what happens when you come to the beginning again?' Alice ventured to ask.

'Suppose we change the subject,' the March Hare interrupted, yawning.

Tea-cup Brindisi

From *The Sorcerer, first performance 1877* | W. S. Gilbert (1836–1911)

Sir Marmaduke:
Eat drink and be gay,
    Banish all worry and sorrow,
Laugh gaily today,
    Weep, if you're sorry, to-morrow!
Come, pass the cup round –
    I will go bail for the liquor;
It's strong, I'll be bound,
    For it was brewed by the vicar!

Chorus:
None so knowing as he
At brewing a jorum of tea,
    Ha! Ha!
A pretty stiff jorum of tea.

The Best Berry

From *The Compleat Angler, 1653–1676*

Izaak Walton (1593–1683), attrib. William Butler (1535–1618)

Piscator:

Indeed my good scholar, we may say of *Angling* as Dr. *Boteler* said of
strawberries: 'Doubtless God could have made a better berry,
but doubtless God never did.'

Seduction with Strawberries

From *Tess of the D'Urbervilles, 1891* | Thomas Hardy (1840–1928)

Tess wished to abridge her visit as much as possible; but the young man was pressing, and she consented to accompany him. He conducted her about the lawns, and flower-beds, and conservatories; and thence to the fruit-garden and greenhouses, where he asked her if she liked strawberries.

'Yes,' said Tess, 'when they come.'

'They are already here.' D'Urberville began gathering specimens of the fruit for her, handing them back to her as he stooped; and, presently, selecting a specially fine product of the 'British Queen' variety, he stood up and held it by the stem to her mouth.

'No – no!' she said quickly, putting her fingers between his hand and her lips. 'I would rather take it in my own hand.'

'Nonsense!' he insisted; and in a slight distress she parted her lips and took it in.

Cutting it Fine

From *The Wind in the Willows, 1908* | Kenneth Grahame (1859–1932)

[The Water Rat:] 'Look here! If you've really nothing else on hand this morning, supposing we drop down the river together, and have a long day of it?'

The Mole waggled his toes from sheer happiness, spread his chest with a sigh of full contentment, and leaned back blissfully into the soft cushions. '*What* a day I'm having!' he said.
'Let us start at once!'

'Hold hard a minute, then!' said the Rat. He looped the painter through a ring in his landing-stage, climbed up into his hole above, and after a short interval reappeared staggering under a fat, wicker luncheon-basket.

'Shove that under your feet,' he observed to the Mole, as he passed it down into the boat. Then he untied the painter and took the sculls again.

'What's inside it?' asked the Mole, wriggling with curiosity.

'There's cold chicken inside it,' replied the Rat briefly; 'coldtonguecoldhamcoldbeefpickledgherkinssaladfrenchrollscress sandwichespottedmeatgingerbeerlemonadesodawater –'

'O stop, stop,' cried the Mole in ecstasies: 'This is too much!'

'Do you really think so?' enquired the Rat seriously. 'It's only what I always take on these little excursions; and the other animals are always telling me that I'm a mean beast and cut it *very* fine!'

Indoors or Out

From *Emma, 1815* | Jane Austen (1775–1817)

Mrs Elton and Mr Knightley:

'I shall wear a large bonnet, and bring one of my little baskets
hanging on my arm. Here, – probably this basket with pink ribbon.
Nothing can be more simple, you see. And Jane will have such
another. There is to be no form or parade – a sort of gipsy party. We
are to walk about your gardens, and gather the strawberries ourselves,
and sit under trees; – and whatever else you may like to provide, it is
to be all out of doors – a table spread in the shade, you know. Every
thing as natural and simple as possible. Is not that your idea?'

'Not quite. My idea of the simple and the natural will be to have
the table spread in the dining-room. The nature and the simplicity
of gentlemen and ladies, with their servants and furniture, I think is
best observed by meals within doors. When you are tired of eating
strawberries in the garden, there shall be cold meat in the house.'

'Well – as you please; only don't have a great set out.'

Open-air Breakfast

From *The Adventures of Tom Sawyer, 1876* | Mark Twain (1835–1910)

They came back to camp wonderfully refreshed, glad-hearted, and ravenous; and they soon had the camp-fire blazing up again. Huck found a spring of clear cold water close by, and the boys made cups of broad oak or hickory leaves, and felt that water, sweetened with such a wildwood charm as that, would be a good enough substitute for coffee. While Joe was slicing bacon for breakfast, Tom and Huck asked him to hold on a minute; they stepped to a promising nook in the river-bank and threw in their lines; almost immediately they had reward. Joe had not had time to get impatient before they were back again with some handsome bass, a couple of sun-perch and a small catfish – provisions enough for quite a family. They fried the fish with the bacon, and were astonished; for no fish had ever seemed so delicious before. They did not know that the quicker a fresh-water fish is on the fire after he is caught the better he is; and they reflected little upon what a sauce open-air sleeping, open-air exercise, bathing, and a large ingredient of hunger make, too.

Drinking Soda Water

From *Five Children and It, 1902* | E. Nesbit (1858–1924)

I do not wish to describe the picnic party on the top of the tower. You can imagine well enough what it is like to carve a chicken and a tongue with a knife that has only one blade and that snapped off short about half-way down. But it was done. Eating with your fingers is greasy and difficult – and paper dishes soon get to look very spotty and horrid. But one thing you can't imagine, and that is how soda-water behaves when you try to drink it straight out of a syphon – especially a quite full one. But if imagination will not help you, experience will, and you can easily try it for yourself if you can get a grown-up to give you the syphon. If you want to have a really thorough experience, put the tube in your mouth and press the handle very suddenly and very hard. You had better do it when you are alone – and out of doors is best for this experiment.

However you eat them, tongue and chicken and new bread are very good things, and no one minds being sprinkled a little with soda-water on a really fine hot day. So that everyone enjoyed the dinner very much indeed, and everyone ate as much as it possibly could: first, because it was extremely hungry; and secondly, because, as I said, tongue and chicken and new bread are very nice.

Satire II

From *Imitations of the Satires of Horace*

Alexander Pope (1688–1744)

To Mr Bethel, lines 1–24

What, and how great, the Virtue and the Art
To live on little with a cheerful heart,
(A doctrine sage, but truly none of mine)
Let's talk, my friends, but talk before we dine:
Not when a gilt Buffet's reflected pride
Turns you from sound Philosophy aside;
Not when from plate to plate your eyeballs roll.
And the brain dances to the mantling bowl.
  Hear BETHEL'S Sermon, one not vers'd in schools.
But strong in sense, and wise without the rules
  Go work, hunt, exercise! (he thus began)
Then scorn a homely dinner, if you can.
Your wine lock'd up, your Butler stroll'd abroad,
Or fish deny'd, (the river yet unthaw'd)
If then plain bread and milk will do the feat,
The pleasure lies in you, and not the meat.
  Preach as I please, I doubt our curious men
Will choose a Pheasant still before a Hen;
Yet hens of Guinea full as good I hold,
Except you eat the feathers, green and gold.
Of carps and mullets why prefer the greats,
(Tho' cut in pieces 'ere my Lord can eat)
Yet for small Turbots such esteem profess?
Because God made these large, the other less.

Going Too Far

From *A Kipper With My Tea: The Harlot of Marseilles*, 1988 |

Alan Davidson (1929–2003)

I know but one and I don't like her at all. I refer, of course, to the meretricious '*bouillabaisse*' which is served in tourist-trapping restaurants around the Old Port of Marseilles, and of which obnoxious echoes are to be found all round the world.

Why be steamed up over this steaming dish? Well, perhaps one shouldn't be; we all have to earn a living, don't we, and maybe exacting high prices from tourists for a tarted up version of what was once a simple fisherman's dish is a venial way of setting about the task. Why be purist, why harp on history, why swim against the tide? Meanings change and *bouillabaisse* is whatever people mean when they use the term, not what a bunch of other people long installed in their graves meant when they used it.

Musing one day along these tolerant and enlightened lines, I came upon an item which sharply restored my rebellious feelings on the subject. There is a book, appropriately called *An Odd Volume of Cookery*, by Louise Lane Morrisey and Marion Lane Sweeney. It was published by the otherwise reputable firm of Houghton Mifflin in Boston in 1949. In it there is a recipe for *bouillabaisse*. This begins: 'Put one can of tomato soup and one can of pea soup in top of double boiler and heat.' The recipe contains no fish, no herbs and no olive oil.

This is going too far.

The Ballad of the Bouillabaisse

William Makepeace Thackeray (1811–1863)

Verses 1–2

A street there is in Paris famous.
    For which no rhyme our language yields,
Rue Neuve des Petits Champs its name is –
    The New Street of the little Fields.
And here's an inn, not rich and splendid,
    But still in comfortable case;
The which in youth I oft attended,
    To eat a bowl of Bouillabaisse.

This Bouillabaisse a noble dish is –
    A sort of soup or broth, or brew,
Or hotchpotch of all sorts of fishes,
    That Greenwich never could out do:
Green herbs, red peppers, mussels, saffron,
    Soles, onions, garlic, roach, and dace:
All these you eat at Terrés tavern.
    In that one dish of Bouillabaisse.

Street Food

From *Picnic, 1981* | Claudia Roden (1936–)

As a child in Cairo I was fascinated by the cries of peddlars and street vendors, itinerant sellers of all types of foods. I waited for each familiar voice to pass under my bedroom window to allay the boredom of my enforced siesta. Sometimes the cry was accompanied by the rattle of pieces of paper twisted around bicycle spokes or by the clinking of glasses or the clanking of brass plates. One man called out every day at two o'clock with a plaintive nasal voice 'Aha awaw!' For a long time I wondered what he sold. When I escaped the siesta and finally saw him, he was selling nothing at all. Perhaps he liked the sound of his cry.

Vendors plying through the streets or standing in the market, carrying their wares on trays placed on tightly coiled cloths on their heads, or in baskets or barrels strapped to their shoulders, were a source of endless fascination. The more perishable the food, the greater the need to dispose of it quickly, the more pressing their cries.

I was impressed by the speed at which they peeled oranges and separated the segments, sprinkled salt on a cucumber and cut a square out of a water-melon before a prospective buyer had made up his mind, eloquently praising the honeysweet virtues of their fruits at the same time.

The Lingering Routine

From *The Innocents Abroad, 1869* | Mark Twain (1835–1910)

We have learned to go through the lingering routine of the table d'hote with patience, with serenity, with satisfaction. We take soup, then wait a few minutes for the fish; a few minutes more and the plates are changed, and the roast beef comes; another change and we take peas; change again and take lentils; change and take snail patties (I prefer grasshoppers); change and take roast chicken and salad; then strawberry pie and ice cream; then green figs, pears, oranges, green almonds, etc.; finally coffee. Wine with every course, of course, being in France. With such a cargo on board, digestion is a slow process, and we must sit long in the cool chambers and smoke – and read French newspapers.

26 June

Shocking or Sensible?

From *A Modest Proposal, 1729* | Jonathan Swift (1667–1745)

A Modest Proposal for preventing the children of Poor People from being a Burthen to their Parents, or the Country, and Making them Beneficial to the Publick.

I shall now therefore humbly propose my own thoughts, which I hope will not be liable to the least objection.

I have been assured by a very knowing *American* of my acquaintance in *London*, that a young healthy Child well Nursed, is, at a year Old, a most delicious nourishing and wholesome Food, whether *Stewed*, *Roasted*, *Baked*, or *Boyled*, and I make no doubt that it will equally serve in a *Fricasie*, or a *Ragoust*.

. . . .

A Child will make two dishes at an Entertainment for Friends, and when the Family dines alone, the fore or hind Quarter will make a reasonable Dish, and seasoned with a little Pepper or Salt, will be very good Boiled on the fourth Day, especially in Winter.

27 June

On Swift's Proposal

From *The English Humourists of the Eighteenth Century:*
Swift, lecture 1851, published 1853

William Makepeace Thackeray (1811–1863)

Could Dick Steele, or Goldsmith, or Fielding, in his most reckless moment of satire, have written anything like the Dean's famous 'Modest Proposal' for eating children? Not one of these but melts at the thoughts of childhood, fondles and caresses it. Mr Dean has no such softness, and enters the nursery with the tread and gaiety of an ogre. 'I have been assured,' says he in the 'Modest Proposal', 'by a very knowing American of my acquaintance in London, that a young healthy child, well nursed, is, at a year old, a most delicious, nourishing, and wholesome food, whether stewed, roasted, baked, or boiled; and I make no doubt it will equally serve in a ragoût.' And taking up this pretty joke, as his way is, he argues it with perfect gravity and logic. He turns and twists this subject in a score of different ways: he hashes it; and he serves it up cold; and he garnishes it; and he relishes it always. He describes the little animal as 'dropped from its dam,' advising that the mother should let it suck plentifully in the last month, so as to render it plump and fat for a good table!

28 June

. . . .

There was a process well known and practised in the Dean's gay days: when a lout entered the coffee-house, the wags proceeded to what they called 'roasting' him. This is roasting a subject with a vengeance. The Dean had a native genius for it. As the 'Almanach des Gourmands' says, *On naît rôtisseur.*

A Comment About Ownership

From *Jerusalem, 2012* | Yotam Ottolenghi (1968–) and Sami Tamimi (1968–)

The futility of arguments about ownership, about provenance, about who and what came first:

Firstly, they are futile because it really doesn't matter. Looking back in time or far afield into distant lands is simply distracting. The beauty of food and eating is that they are rooted in the now. Food is a basic, hedonistic pleasure, a sensual instinct we all share and revel in. It is a shame to spoil it.

Secondly, you can always search further back in time. Hummus for example, a highly explosive subject, is undeniably a staple of the local Palestinian population, but it was also a permanent feature on dinner tables of Allepian Jews who have lived in Syria for millennia and then arrived in Jerusalem in the 1950s and 1960s. Who is more deserving of calling hummus their own? Neither. Nobody 'owns' a dish because it is very likely that someone else cooked it before them and another person before that.

29 June

Thirdly, and this is the most crucial point, in this soup of a city it is completely impossible to find out who invented this delicacy and who brought that one with them. The food cultures are mashed and fused together in a way that is impossible to unravel. They interact all the time and influence each other constantly so nothing is pure any more. In fact, nothing ever was. Jerusalem was never an isolated bastion. Over millennia it has seen countless immigrants, occupiers, visitors and merchants – all bringing food and recipes from four corners of the earth.

As a result, as much as we try to attribute foods to nations, to ascertain the origin of a dish, we often end up discovering a dozen other dishes that are extremely similar, that work with the same ingredients and the same principles to make a final result that is just ever so slightly different, a variation on a theme.

29 June

An Air of Profusion

From *The Road to Oxiana, 1937* | Robert Byron (1905–1941)

Mazar-i-Sherif, Afghanistan

Judged by Russian standards, which differ from ours, the food was
not really profuse; indeed how could it be? though they had bought,
at considerable expense we discovered afterwards, the last sardines
in the town. But it had that *air* of profusion which Russians always
create about them, and as new guests kept wandering in, and new
tables were brought, and new chairs, and the children hopped up
on people's laps, the dishes kept pace and were still as full as ever of
the sardines from India, paprika from Russia, fresh meat with onion
salad, and bread. A decanter of yellow vodka, in which fruit was
swimming, was endlessly replenished. The Russians, who gulped
it off in cups, complained furiously of our slow sipping. But that
was only at first.

30 June

JULY

The Mellowing Influence of Good Food

Let's be Merry

From *Letter to Maria Gisborne* | Percy Bysshe Shelley (1792–1822)

Leghorn, *July 1, 1820*
Lines 302–307
Though we eat little flesh and drink no wine,
Yet let's be merry: we'll have tea and toast;
Custards for supper, and an endless host
Of syllabubs and jellies and mince-pies,
And other such lady-like luxuries, –
Feasting on which we will philosophize!

To Distill Walnut-water

From *The Art of Cookery Made Plain and Easy, 1747*

Hannah Glasse (1708–1770)

Take a Peck of fine green Walnuts, bruise them well in a large
Mortar, put them in a Pan, with a Handful of Balm bruised, and
put two Quarts of good French Brandy to them, cover them close,
and let them lye three Days; the next Day distill them in a cold Still,
from this quantity draw three Quarts, which you may do in a Day.

How to Use this Ordinary Still:
You must lay Wood Ashes thick at the Bottom, on that the Plate,
then the Iron-pan, which you are to fill with your Walnuts and
Liquor, then put on the Head of the Still, make a pretty brisk Fire
till the Still begins to drop, then slacken it so as just to have enough
to keep the Still at Work, and mind all the Time to keep a wet Cloth
all over the Head of the Still all the Time it is at Work, and always
observe not to let the Still work longer than the Liquor is good, and
take great Care you don't burn the Still; and thus you may distil what
you please. If you draw the Still too far it will burn, and give your
Liquor a bad Taste.

Meat and Drink on the Same Tree

From *The Coral Island, 1857* | R. M. Ballantyne (1825–1894)

Jack halts under the shade of a cocoa-nut tree:

'You said you were thirsty just a minute ago; now, jump up that tree and bring down a nut, – not a ripe one, bring a green, unripe one.'

Peterkin looked surprised, but, seeing that Jack was in earnest, he obeyed.

'Now, cut a hole in it with your penknife, and clap it to your mouth, old fellow,' said Jack.

Peterkin did as he was directed, and we both burst into uncontrollable laughter at the changes that instantly passed over his expressive countenance. No sooner had he put the nut to his mouth, and thrown back his head in order to catch what came out of it, than his eyes opened to twice their ordinary size with astonishment, while his throat moved vigorously in the act of swallowing. Then a smile and look of intense delight overspread his face, except, indeed, the mouth, which, being firmly fixed to the hole in the nut, could not take part in the expression; but he endeavoured to make up for this by winking at us excessively with his right eye. At length he stopped, and, drawing a long breath, exclaimed –

'Nectar! perfect nectar! – I say, Jack, you're a Briton – the best fellow I ever met in my life. Only taste that! –' said he, turning to me and holding the nut to my mouth. I immediately drank, and certainly I was much surprised at the delightful liquid that flowed copiously down my throat. It was extremely cool, and had a sweet taste, mingled with acid; in fact, it was the likest thing to lemonade I ever tasted, and was most grateful and refreshing. I handed the nut to Jack, who, after tasting it, said, 'Now, Peterkin, you unbeliever! I never saw or tasted a cocoa-nut in my life before, except those sold in shops at home; but I once read that the green nuts contain that stuff, and you see it is true.'

'And pray,' asked Peterkin, 'what sort of 'stuff' does the ripe nut contain?'

'A hollow kernel,' answered Jack, 'with a liquid like milk in it; but it does not satisfy thirst so well as hunger. It is very wholesome food I believe.'

'Meat and drink on the same tree!' cried Peterkin.

Meet the Dish of the Day

From *The Restaurant at the End of the Universe, 1980*

Douglas Adams (1952–2001)

The waiter approached.

'Would you like to see the menu,' he said, or would you like to meet the Dish of the Day?'

'Huh?' said Ford.

'Huh?' said Arthur.

'Huh?' said Trillian.

'That's cool,' said Zaphod, 'we'll meet the meat.'

. . . .

A large dairy animal approached Zaphod Beeblebrox's table, a large fat meaty quadruped of the bovine type with large watery eyes, small horns and what might almost have been an ingratiating smile on its lips.

'Good evening,' it lowed and sat back heavily on its haunches, 'I am the main Dish of the Day. May I interest you in parts of my body?' It harrumphed and gurgled a bit, wriggled its hind quarters into a more comfortable position and gazed peacefully at them.

A Nightmare That Leads to Lobster

From *The Man Who Was Thursday, 1908*

G. K. Chesterton (1874–1936)

'Will you take a little supper?' asked Gregory politely. 'The *pâté de foie gras* is not good here, but I can recommend the game.'

Syme received the remark with stolidity, imagining it to be a joke. Accepting the vein of humour, he said, with a well-bred indifference –

'Oh, bring me some lobster mayonnaise.'

To his indescribable astonishment, the man only said 'Certainly, sir!' and went away apparently to get it.

'What will you drink?' resumed Gregory, with the same careless yet apologetic air. 'I shall only have a *crème de menthe* myself; I have dined. But the champagne can really be trusted. Do let me start you with a half-bottle of Pommery at least?'

'Thank you!' said the motionless Syme. 'You are very good.'

His further attempts at conversation, somewhat disorganised in themselves, were cut short finally as by a thunderbolt by the actual appearance of the lobster. Syme tasted it, and found it particularly good. Then he suddenly began to eat with great rapidity and appetite.

'Excuse me if I enjoy myself rather obviously!' he said to Gregory, smiling. 'I don't often have the luck to have a dream like this. It is new to me for a nightmare to lead to a lobster. It is commonly the other way.'

At Tea

Thomas Hardy (1840–1928)

The kettle descants in a cosy drone,
And the young wife looks in her husband's face,
And then at her guest's, and shows in her own
Her sense that she fills an envied place;
And the visiting lady is all abloom,
And says there was never so sweet a room.

And the happy young housewife does not know
That the woman beside her was first his choice,
Till the fates ordained it could not be so …
Betraying nothing in look or voice
The guest sits smiling and sips her tea,
And he throws her a stray glance yearningly.

Second Cabin Class

From *The Amateur Emigrant, 1895*

Robert Louis Stevenson (1850–1894)

At breakfast we had a choice between tea and coffee for beverage; a choice not easy to make, the two were so surprisingly alike. I found that I could sleep after the coffee and lay awake after the tea; which is proof conclusive of some chemical disparity; and even by the palate I could distinguish a smack of snuff in the former from a flavour of boiling and dish-cloths in the second. As a matter of fact, I have seen passengers, after many sips, still doubting which had been supplied them. In the way of eatables at the same meal we were gloriously favoured; for in addition to porridge, which was common to all, we had Irish stew, sometimes a bit of fish, and sometimes rissoles. The dinner of soup, roast fresh beef, boiled salt junk, and potatoes was, I believe, exactly common to the steerage and the second cabin; only I have heard it rumoured that our potatoes were of a superior brand; and twice a week, on pudding days, instead of duff, we had a saddle-bag filled with currants under the name of a plum-pudding. At tea we were served with some broken meat from the saloon; sometimes in the comparatively elegant form of spare patties or rissoles; but as a general thing mere chicken-bones and flakes of fish, neither hot nor cold. If these were not the scrapings of plates their looks belied them sorely; yet we were all too hungry to be proud, and fell to these leavings greedily. These, the bread, which was excellent, and the soup and porridge which were both good, formed my whole diet throughout the voyage; so that except for the broken meat and the convenience of a table I might as well have been in the steerage outright. Had they given me porridge again in the evening I should have been perfectly contented with the fare. As it was, with a few biscuits and some whisky and water before turning in, I kept my body going and my spirits up to the mark.

7 July

A Very Special Thing

From *Kipps, 1905* | H. G. Wells (1866–1946)

Kipps made a very special thing of his breakfast. Daily once hopeless dreams came true then. It had been customary in the Emporium to supplement Shalford's generous, indeed unlimited, supply of bread and butter-substitute, by private purchases, and this had given Kipps very broad, artistic conceptions of what the meal might be. Now there would be a cutlet or so or a mutton chop – this splendour Buggins had reported from the great London clubs – haddock, kipper, whiting or fish-balls, eggs, boiled or scrambled, or eggs and bacon, kidney also frequently and sometimes liver. Amidst a garland of such themes, sausages, black and white puddings, bubble-and-squeak, fried cabbage and scallops came and went. Always as camp followers came potted meat in all varieties, cold bacon, German sausage, brawn, marmalade and two sorts of jam, and when he had finished these he would sit among his plates and smoke a cigarette and look at all these dishes crowded round him with a beatific approval. It was his principal meal.

An Hour of Joy

From *Sons and Lovers, 1913* | D. H. Lawrence (1885–1930)

He [Walter Morel] always made his own breakfast. Being a man who
rose early and had plenty of time he did not, as some miners do, drag
his wife out of bed at six o'clock. At five, sometimes earlier, he woke,
got straight out of bed, and went downstairs. When she could not
sleep, his wife lay waiting for this time, as for a period of peace. The
only real rest seemed to be when he was out of the house.

He went downstairs in his shirt and then struggled into his pit-
trousers, which were left on the hearth to warm all night. There was
always a fire, because Mrs Morel raked. And the first sound in the
house was the bang, bang of the poker against the raker, as Morel
smashed the remainder of the coal to make the kettle, which was
filled and left on the hob, finally boil. His cup and knife and fork,
all he wanted except just the food, was laid ready on the table on
a newspaper. Then he got his breakfast, made the tea, packed the
bottom of the doors with rugs to shut out the draught, piled a big
fire, and sat down to an hour of joy. He toasted his bacon on a fork
and caught the drops of fat on his bread; then he put the rasher on
his thick slice of bread, and cut off chunks with a clasp-knife, poured
his tea into his saucer, and was happy. With his family about, meals
were never so pleasant. He loathed a fork: it is a modern introduction
which has still scarcely reached common people. What Morel
preferred was a clasp-knife. Then, in solitude, he ate and drank,
often sitting, in cold weather, on a little stool with his back to the
warm chimney-piece, his food on the fender, his cup on the hearth.
And then he read the last night's newspaper – what of it he could –
spelling it over laboriously. He preferred to keep the blinds down and
the candle lit even when it was daylight; it was the habit of the mine.

Peas

Anon

I eat my peas with honey,
I've done it all my life,
It makes the peas taste funny,
But it keeps them on the knife.

10 July

Eating Peas

From *Cranford, 1853* | Elizabeth Gaskell (1810–1865)

When the ducks and green peas came, we looked at each other in dismay; we had only two-pronged, black-handled forks. It is true the steel was as bright as silver; but what were we to do? Miss Matty picked up her peas, one by one, on the point of the prongs, much as Aminé ate her grains of rice after her previous feast with the Ghoul. Miss Pole sighed over her delicate young peas as she left them on one side of her plate untasted, for they *would* drop between the prongs. I looked at my host: the peas were going wholesale into his capacious mouth, shovelled up by his large round-ended knife. I saw, I imitated, I survived! My friends, in spite of my precedent, could not muster up courage enough to do an ungenteel thing; and, if Mr Holbrook had not been so heartily hungry, he would probably have seen that the good peas went away almost untouched.

11 July

The Potato-shaped Space

From *Cooking in a Bedsitter, 1961, 1963*

Katharine Whitehorn (1928–2021)

Most of us have a potato-shaped space inside that must be filled at every meal, if not by potatoes, then by something equally filling – rice, bread, spaghetti, macaroni and so on. This is a big problem for people coming hungrily home; for this is the part of the meal that often takes longest to cook, and it is often difficult to work in the cooking of potatoes or rice with other things. Where I could, I have tried to add instructions for adding potatoes or rice even to dishes in which they do not figure by nature; but anyone who cares greatly about speed would do well either to get into the habit of eating bread with a meal instead; or of cooking several days' supply of potatoes at a time, keeping them covered in the meantime, and just heating up a few in each new dish. Rice, too, will heat up all right with a little extra water, though if it stands for more than a day there will be some bits that have gone brittle and should be thrown out. By the same token, those who (rightly) care about eating green vegetables every day should get into the way of eating separate salads with their meals: that way, they may avoid having to cook an extra vegetable every time they feel they are running short on essential vitamins.

Potatoes

From *Three Men in a Boat, 1889* | Jerome K. Jerome (1859–1927)

Harris and I started to peel the potatoes. I should never have thought that peeling potatoes was such an undertaking. The job turned out to be the biggest thing of its kind that I had ever been in. We began cheerfully, one might almost say skittishly, but our light-heartedness was gone by the time the first potato was finished. The more we peeled, the more peel there seemed to be left on; by the time we had got all the peel off and all the eyes out, there was no potato left – at least none worth speaking of. George came and had a look at it – it was about the size of a pea-nut. He said:

'Oh, that won't do! You're wasting them. You must scrape them.'

So we scraped them, and that was harder work than peeling. They are such an extraordinary shape, potatoes – all bumps and warts and hollows. We worked steadily for five-and-twenty minutes, and did four potatoes. Then we struck. We said we should require the rest of the evening for scraping ourselves.

I never saw such a thing as potato-scraping for making a fellow in a mess. It seemed difficult to believe that the potato-scrapings in which Harris and I stood, half smothered, could have come off four potatoes. It shows you what can be done with economy and care.

George said it was absurd to have only four potatoes in an Irish stew, so we washed half-a-dozen or so more, and put them in without peeling.

The English Apricot

From *The Anatomy of Dessert, 1929* | Edward Bunyard (1878–1939)

The perfect Apricot is not easily come by; too often we find a mealy cotton-wool texture where we looked for a translucent and melting flesh.

Too much water, lack of sun and air, are two of the faults which require correction. At its best the Apricot has a certain Eastern lusciousness, a touch of the exotic which comes strangely into our homely country. In some Persian Palace whose quiet garden hears only the tinkle of a fountain it would seem to find its right setting, fitly waiting on a golden dish for some languid Sharazade. But even in the sun-warmed Midi it is not always grown to perfection, and much of the fruit which enters this country from abroad is quite unworthy. Gathered too early, they do not even look like apricots. Pale cream is their wear, in place of the wine-stained gold that they should show. Those from Angoumois are often good, and in their native country supreme. We can, however, produce as good a fruit in England, given a warm wall, thoughtful culture, and a favourable season.

Sandwiches and Currant Buns

From *The Housing Lark, 1965* | Sam Selvon (1923–1994)

On the green banks of old father Thames most of the excursionists were scattered, getting ready for lunch.

'What did you bring?' Charlie asked Maisie.

'Well, I have some cucumber and cheese sandwiches, four currant buns, and a Thermos of tea,' Maisie say.

Charlie groan. All around him pot cover flying off and some heavy yam and sweet potato putting in appearance. Leg of ham, leg of lamb, chicken leg and chicken wing and chicken breast. One woman have a big wooden spoon dishing out peas and rice from the biggest pot Maisie ever seen in her life, except for a few she see in the palace, when they visit the kitchen, and she selling a plate for two and six. A lot of people queuing up with paper plates.

'I think I'll have a plate of that.' Charlie say, throwing decorum to the winds. 'You could have all the sandwiches, and the currant buns, and the Thermos of tea.'

15 July

A Picnic

From *Audley Court* | Alfred, Lord Tennyson (1809–1892)

There, on a slope of orchard, Francis laid
A damask napkin wrought with horse and hound,
Brought out a dusky loaf that smelt of home,
And, half-cut-down, a pasty costly-made,
Where quail and pigeon, lark and leveret lay,
Like fossils of the rock, with golden yolks
Imbedded and injellied; last, with these,
A flask of cider from his father's vats,
Prime, which I knew; and so we sat and eat
And talk'd old matters over; who was dead,
Who married, who was like to be, and how
The races went, and who would rent the hall:
Then touch'd upon the game, how scarce it was
This season; glancing thence, discuss'd the farm,
The four-field system, and the price of grain;
And struck upon the corn-laws, where we split,
And came again together on the king
With heated faces; till he laugh'd aloud.

A Picnic with the Sea Rat

From *The Wind in the Willows, 1908* | Kenneth Grahame (1859–1932)

'That reminds me,' said the polite Water Rat; 'you happened to mention that you were hungry, and I ought to have spoken earlier. Of course, you will stop and take your midday meal with me? My hole is close by; it is some time past noon, and you are very welcome to whatever there is.'

'Now I call that kind and brotherly of you,' said the Sea Rat. 'I was indeed hungry when I sat down, and ever since I inadvertently happened to mention shell-fish, my pangs have been extreme. But couldn't you fetch it along out here? I am none too fond of going under hatches, unless I'm obliged to; and then, while we eat, I could tell you more concerning my voyages and the pleasant life I lead – at least, it is very pleasant to me, and by your attention I judge it commends itself to you; whereas if we go indoors it is a hundred to one that I shall presently fall asleep.'

'That is indeed an excellent suggestion,' said the Water Rat, and hurried off home. There he got out the luncheon-basket and packed a simple meal, in which, remembering the stranger's origin and preferences, he took care to include a yard of long French bread, a sausage out of which the garlic sang, some cheese which lay down and cried, and a long-necked straw-covered flask wherein lay bottled sunshine shed and garnered on far Southern slopes. Thus laden, he returned with all speed, and blushed for pleasure at the old seaman's commendations of his taste and judgment, as together they unpacked the basket and laid out the contents on the grass by the roadside.

TV Dinners

From *The Bachelor Home Companion, 1987* |

P. J. O'Rourke (1947–2022)

TV dinners aren't so bad if you remember to peel the foil back from the custard thingy.

A Gingerbread House

From *The Country of Pointed Firs, 1896* | Sarah Orne Jewett
(1849–1909)

The most renowned essay in cookery on the tables was a model of
the old Bowden house made of durable gingerbread, with all the
windows and doors in the right places, and sprigs of genuine lilac
set at the front. It must have been baked in sections, in one of the last
of the great brick ovens, and fastened together on the morning
of the day. There was a general sigh when this fell into ruin at the
feast's end, and it was shared by a great part of the assembly, not
without seriousness, and as if it were a pledge and token of loyalty.
I met the maker of the gingerbread house, which had called up lively
remembrances of a childish story. She had the gleaming eye of an
enthusiast and a look of high ideals.

'I could just as well have made it all of frosted cake,' she said, 'but
'twouldn't have been the right shade; the old house, as you observe,
was never painted, and I concluded that plain gingerbread would
represent it best. It wasn't all I expected it would be,' she said sadly,
as many an artist had said before her of his work.

The Little House

From *Hansel and Gretel, 1812*

Collected by The Brothers Grimm, Jacob (1785–1863) and Wilhelm (1786–1859)

Translated by Andrew Lang (1844–1912) in *The Blue Fairy Book*, 1889

Hansel and Gretel follow the snow-white bird:

They followed it and came to a little house, on the roof of which it perched; and when they came quite near they saw that the cottage was made of bread and roofed with cakes, while the window was made of transparent sugar. 'Now we'll set to,' said Hansel, 'and have a regular blow-out. I'll eat a bit of the roof, and you, Gretel, can eat some of the window, which you'll find a sweet morsel.' Hansel stretched up his hand and broke off a little bit of the roof to see what it was like, and Gretel went to the casement and began to nibble at it. Thereupon a shrill voice called out from the room inside:

'Nibble, nibble, little mouse,

Who's nibbling my house?'

The children answered:

''Tis Heaven's own child,

The tempest wild,'

and went on eating, without putting themselves about. Hansel, who thoroughly appreciated the roof, tore down a big bit of it, while Gretel pushed out a whole round window-pane, and sat down the better to enjoy it. Suddenly the door opened, and an ancient dame leaning on a staff hobbled out. Hansel and Gretel were so terrified that they let what they had in their hands fall. But the old woman shook her head and said: 'Oh, ho! you dear children, who led you here? Just come in and stay with me, no ill shall befall you.' She took them both by the hand and let them into the house, and laid a most sumptuous dinner before them – milk and sugared pancakes, with apples and nuts. After they had finished, two beautiful little white beds were prepared for them, and when Hansel and Gretel lay down in them they felt as if they had got into heaven.

Dining Alone

From *The Awakening, 1899* | Kate Chopin (1850–1904)

When Edna was at last alone, she breathed a big, genuine sigh
of relief:

Even the kitchen assumed a sudden interesting character which
she had never before perceived. She went in to give directions to the
cook, to say that the butcher would have to bring much less meat,
that they would require only half their usual quantity of bread,
of milk and groceries. She told the cook that she herself would be
greatly occupied during Mr. Pontellier's absence, and she begged
her to take all thought and responsibility of the larder upon her
own shoulders.

That night Edna dined alone. The candelabra, with a few candles
in the center of the table, gave all the light she needed. Outside the
circle of light in which she sat, the large dining-room looked solemn
and shadowy. The cook, placed upon her mettle, served a delicious
repast – a luscious tenderloin broiled *à point*. The wine tasted good;
the *marron glacé* seemed to be just what she wanted. It was so
pleasant, too, to dine in a comfortable *peignoir*.

My Mother

From *Tender at the Bone, 1998* | Ruth Reichl (1948–)

'Oh, it's just a little mold,' I can remember her saying on the many occasions she scraped the blue fuzzy stuff off some concoction before serving what was left for dinner. She had an iron stomach and was incapable of understanding that other people did not.

This taught me many things. The first was that food could be dangerous, especially to those who loved it. I took this very seriously. My parents entertained a great deal, and before I was ten I had appointed myself guardian of the guests. My mission was to keep Mom from killing anybody who came to dinner.

Her friends seemed surprisingly unaware that they took their lives in their hands each time they ate with us. They chalked their ailments up to the weather, the flu, or one of my mother's more unusual dishes. 'No more sea urchins for me,' I imagined Burt Langner saying to his wife, Ruth, after a dinner at our house, 'they just don't agree with me.' Little did he know that it was not the sea urchins that had made him ill, but the bargain beef my mother had found so irresistible.

Remarks

From *Simple French Cooking for English Homes, 1923*

Xavier Marcel Boulestin (1878–1943)

Do not be afraid to talk about food. Food which is worth eating is worth discussing. And there is the occult power of words which somehow will develop its qualities.

. . . .

A good cook is not necessarily a good woman with an even temper. Some allowance should be made for the artistic temperament.

. . . .

One cannot underrate the mellowing influence of good food on civilised beings. Hence the 'business luncheons'.

. . . .

Give your friends 'something' to drink – not lemonade, which is worse than nothing, nothing meaning plain water.

. . . .

Always buy fruit yourself. Do not order by telephone; you should see what you are buying. Go and pick the best. If you greengrocer does not like your ways, do not change them – change him.

. . . .

Do not be afraid of simplicity. If you have a cold chicken for supper, why cover it with a tasteless white sauce which makes it look like a pretentious dish on the buffet table at some fancy dress ball.

23 July

The Kitchen

From *Good Things, 1971* | Jane Grigson (1928–1990)

Many families, not just the housewife, now do the cooking between them, and enjoy a protracted sociable meal as an opportunity for talking and discussing with an enthusiasm that was not encouraged at dinner parties thirty years ago. Cooking something delicious is really much more satisfactory than painting pictures or throwing pots. At least for most of us. Food has the tact to disappear, leaving room and opportunity for masterpieces to come. The mistakes don't hang on the walls or stand on the shelves to reproach you for ever. It follows from this that kitchens should be thought of as the centre of the house. They need above all space for talking, playing, bringing up children, sewing, having a meal, reading, sitting and thinking. One may have to walk about a bit but where's the harm in that? Everything will not be shipshape, galley-fashion, but it's in this kind of place that good food has flourished. It's from this secure retreat that the exploration of man's curious and close relationship with food, beyond the point of nourishment, can start.

The Garden of Eden

From *Picnic, 1981* | Claudia Roden (1936–)

My own experience of the Garden of Eden was in the Seychelles islands.

Whiffs from ripe mangoes and pawpaws, still hanging on the trees, mingled with the smell of bananas simmering in coconut milk and the fermenting juice of sugar cane. It was difficult to tell if the scent of vanilla came from the fragile pods dangling on their climbing stalks or from the sweet potato and yam pudding in the pot.

Scents became confused with colours and sounds. A hundred shades of green were pierced by scarlet flowered flamboyants and pale mauve bougainvillaeas. The gentle bubbling of the daube and the crackling of the fire were accompanied by the rustling of palms and the chattering chorus of little red cardinals, warblers and sunbirds.

Lunch was prepared in the open, for all to see. Exchanges were shouted about the contents of the pots which were fondly watched over by the women. To constant giggling and laughter I accepted every invitation to taste. I tried peppery fish soup, the contents of which had been found caught in the twisted bamboo trap now resting by the fire. A coconut fallen not far away had provided the liquor for the bread-fruit daube. Black fresh-water prawns, caught in the stream by a little boy were turning red on dying embers. A sweet potato melted in the ashes. Indian Ocean Creole food, amid the trees and the birds, was an assault on all the senses; I had to hold my breath to eat. Today the smell is still in my nostrils, the taste still on my tongue.

Grace Before Meat

From *Essays of Elia: Grace Before Dinner, 1823* | Charles Lamb
(1775–1834)

The custom of saying grace at meals had, probably, its origin in the early times of the world, and the hunter-state of man, when dinners were precarious things, and a full meal was something more than a common blessing! when a belly-full was a wind-fall, and looked like a special providence. In the shouts and triumphal songs with which, after a season of sharp abstinence, a lucky booty of deer's or goat's flesh would naturally be ushered home, existed, perhaps, the germ of the modern grace. It is not otherwise easy to be understood, why the blessing of food – the act of eating – should have had a particular expression of thanksgiving annexed to it, distinct from that implied and silent gratitude with which we are expected to enter upon the enjoyment of the many other various gifts and good things of existence.

I own that I am disposed to say grace upon twenty other occasions in the course of the day besides my dinner. I want a form for setting out upon a pleasant walk, for a moonlight ramble, for a friendly meeting, or a solved problem. Why have we none for books, those spiritual repasts – a grace before Milton – a grace before Shakspeare – a devotional exercise proper to be said before reading the Fairy Queen?

The Selkirk Grace

Robert Burns (1759–1796)

Some hae meat an canna eat,
    And some wad eat that want it;
But we hae meat, and we can eat,
    And sae the Lord be thankit.

High Living

From *Sailing Alone around the World, 1900*

Joshua Slocum (1844–1909)

28th July was exceptionally fine. The wind from the northwest was
light and the air balmy. I overhauled my wardrobe, and bent on a
white shirt against nearing some coasting-packet with genteel folk
on board. I also did some washing to get the salt out of my clothes.
After it all I was hungry, so I made a fire and very cautiously stewed
a dish of pears and set them carefully aside till I had made a pot of
delicious coffee, for both of which I could afford sugar and cream.
But the crowning dish of all was a fish-hash, and there was enough
of it for two. I was in good health again, and my appetite was simply
ravenous. While I was dining I had a large onion over the double
lamp stewing for a luncheon later in the day. High living to-day!

28 July

Tasting Books

From *Essays: Of Studies, 1597* | Francis Bacon (1561–1626)

Some books are to be tasted, others to be swallowed, and some few
to be chewed and digested. That is, some books are only to be read in
parts; others to be read but cursorily; and some few to be read wholly,
and with diligence and concentration.

The Habits of Cake

From *Anne of Green Gables, 1908* | L. M. Montgomery (1874–1942)

The new minister and his wife are invited to tea:

'Everything is ready, Diana, except my cake which I'm to make in the morning, and the baking-powder biscuits which Marilla will make just before teatime. I assure you, Diana, that Marilla and I have had a busy two days of it. It's such a responsibility having a minister's family to tea. I never went through such an experience before. You should just see our pantry. It's a sight to behold. We're going to have jellied chicken and cold tongue. We're to have two kinds of jelly, red and yellow, and whipped cream and lemon pie, and cherry pie, and three kinds of cookies, and fruit cake, and Marilla's famous yellow plum preserves that she keeps especially for ministers, and pound cake and layer cake, and biscuits as aforesaid; and new bread and old both, in case the minister is dyspeptic and can't eat new. Mrs Lynde says ministers are dyspeptic, but I don't think Mr. Allan has been a minister long enough for it to have had a bad effect on him. I just grow cold when I think of my layer cake. Oh, Diana, what if it shouldn't be good! I dreamed last night that I was chased all around by a fearful goblin with a big layer cake for a head.'

'It'll be good, all right,' assured Diana, who was a very comfortable sort of friend. 'I'm sure that piece of the one you made that we had for lunch in Idlewild two weeks ago was perfectly elegant.'

'Yes; but cakes have such a terrible habit of turning out bad just when you especially want them to be good,' sighed Anne.

Loaves and Fishes

Matthew 14: 15–21 | The King James Bible, 1611

15: And when it was evening, his disciples came to him, saying, 'This is a desert place, and the time is now past; send the multitude away, that they may go into the villages, and buy themselves victuals.'

16: But Jesus said unto them, 'They need not depart; give ye them to eat.'

17: And they say unto him, 'We have here but five loaves, and two fishes.'

18: He said, 'Bring them hither to me.'

19: And he commanded the multitude to sit down on the grass, and took the five loaves, and the two fishes, and looking up to heaven, he blessed, and brake, and gave the loaves to his disciples, and the disciples to the multitude.

20: And they did all eat, and were filled: and they took up of the fragments that remained twelve baskets full.

21: And they that had eaten were about five thousand men, beside women and children.

AUGUST

An Exquisite Scent of Olives and Oil

Cucumber

From *A Tour of the Hebrides, 1785* | James Boswell (1740–1795)

Samuel Johnson (1709–1784)

Dr Johnson:

It has been a common saying of physicians in England, that a cucumber should be well sliced, and dressed with pepper and vinegar, and then thrown out, as good for nothing.

1 August

Snozzcumbers

From *The BFG, 1982* | Roald Dahl (1916–1990)

'But if you don't eat people like all the other,' Sophie said, 'then what do you live on?'

'That is a squelching tricky problem around here,' the BFG answered. 'In this shloshflunking Giant Country, happy eats like pineapples and pigwinkles is simply not growing. Nothing is growing except one extremely icky-poo vegetable. It is called a snozzcumber.'

'The snozzcumber!' cried Sophie. 'There's no such thing.'

The BFG looked at Sophie and smiled, showing about twenty of his square white teeth. 'Yesterday,' he said, 'we was not believing in giants, was we? Today we is not believing in snozzcumbers. Just because we happen not to have actually seen something with our own two little winkles, we think it is not existing.'

. . . .

The BFG flung open a massive cupboard and took out the weirdest-looking thing Sophie had ever seen. It was about half as long again as an ordinary man but was much thicker. It was as thick around its girth as a perambulator. It was black with white stripes along its length. And it was covered all over with coarse knobbles.

'Here is the repulsant snozzcumber!' cried the BFG, waving it about. 'I squoggle it! I mispise it! I dispunge it! But because I is refusing to gobble up human beans like the other giants, I must spend my life guzzling up icky-poo snozzcumbers instead. If I don't, I will be nothing but skin and groans.'

Pomona

William Morris (1834–1896)

I am the ancient Apple-Queen,
As once I was so am I now.
For evermore a hope unseen,
Betwixt the blossom and the bough.

Ah, where's the river's hidden Gold!
And where the windy grave of Troy?
Yet come I as I came of old,
From out the hearts of Summer's joy.

Tinned Fruit

From *Toast, 2003* | Nigel Slater (1956–)

We lived in a world of tinned fruit. There were tinned peaches for high days and holidays, fruit cocktail for every day and tinned pears for my father who said they were better than fresh. There were apricots and segments of mandarin oranges that turned up in orange jelly and, once, figs, which nobody really liked. On one occasion we tried mango but my father said it tasted fishy. I wasn't allowed to try it. 'You won't like it.'

The highlight was not the peaches we ate when someone special came to tea, but the diced delights of fruit cocktail. Grey cubes of grainy pear, semi-cubes of peach, ridged chunks of pineapple and, best of all, lipstick-red maraschino cherries all floating in a divinely sweet syrup. We ate it from red Pyrex dishes, the fruit poking up like a multicoloured rockery in a pool of Ideal milk.

'If you really want to, dear,' was my mother's answer for anything I wanted to do that she would rather I didn't. This was her stock answer to my question: Can I make a fruit sundae? By make I mean assemble. My fruit sundae was a gloriously over-the-top mess of strawberry ice cream, tinned fruit cocktail, maraschino cherries and any nuts I could lay my hands on. I always saved a cherry for the centre. Believe me when I tell you it was the envy of all who set eyes upon it.

Gooseberry Competitions

From *A Kipper With My Tea: On the Trail of Giant Gooseberries, 1986* | Alan Davidson (1929–2003)

On 6 August last year the geese at the village pub in Egton Bridge, North Yorkshire, became over-excited and paraded up and down the grass in a manner even more ridiculous than usual. They must have been infected by the local excitement over the annual Egton Bridge Old Gooseberry Competition, held on that day. No doubt they will be infected again on 5 August this year, for the competition is an annual event which has been reputedly going on since 1800 and shows no signs of dying out. On the contrary, last year's event, which I attended, saw the establishment of a new Egton Bridge record: a berry weighing nearly two ounces (60g).

Gooseberry competitions are not recommended for thrill-seekers; but for those who relish quaint and out-of-the-way aspects of English rural life, uncluttered by busloads of tourists, they are perfect.

The growing and eating of gooseberries is very much a British activity. I say 'British' because the Scots as well as the English have the right climate and plenty of enthusiasm. But the craze which began in the eighteenth century for growing giant gooseberries was really an English one.

The gooseberry bush, unlike the apple tree, can be grown in a very small garden. So it provided an outlet for the horticultural enthusiasm of the workers living in small terraces houses, usually with a tiny garden attached, in the growing cities of the Industrial Revolution. Manchester in Lancashire was one such, and it was there, in 1786, that the first national register of gooseberry competitions was published. But the centre of gooseberry gravity shifted eventually to Cheshire and Yorkshire, and it is in those two counties that the ten surviving competitions are held.

How to Eat Ice Cream

From *Meaty, 2020* | Samantha Irby (1980–)

Step 1: Procure pint of Ben & Jerry's Mint Chocolate Cookie
ice cream.

Step 2: Leave said ice cream on counter for several minutes to soften
while keening impatiently.

Step 3: Eat ice cream a quarter of the way down, vow to stop.

Step 4: Contemplate returning ice cream to freezer.

Step 5: Swear not to consume more than half this ice cream tonight.

Step 6: Okay, but if I don't finish it all that's still a win, right?

Step 7: (Buries empty carton under various trash in waste-basket,
head hung in shame.)

Evenings at Cotrone

From *Old Calabria, 1915* | Norman Douglas (1868–1952)

I usually take a final dip in the sea, at this time of the evening. After that, it is advisable to absorb an ice or two – they are excellent, at Cotrone – and a glass of Strega liqueur, to ward off the effects of over-work. Next, a brief promenade through the clean, well-lighted streets and now populous streets, or along the boulevard Margherita to view the rank and fashion taking the air by the murmuring waves, under the cliff-like battlements of Charles the Fifth's castle; and so to dinner.

This meal marks the termination of my daily tasks; nothing serious is allowed to engage my attention, once that repast is ended; I call for a chair and sit down at one of the small marble-topped tables in the open street and watch the crowd as it floats around me, smoking a Neapolitan cigar and imbibing, alternately, ices and black coffee until, towards midnight, a final bottle of *vino di Cirò* is uncorked – fit seal for the labours of the day.

Haggis

From *The Expedition of Humphry Clinker, 1771*

Tobias Smollett (1721–1771)

Edinburgh, Aug. 8

To Sir Watkin Phillips, Bart. of Jesus college, Oxon

I must own, some of their dishes are savoury, and even delicate;
but I am not yet Scotchman enough to relish their singed sheep's-
head and haggice, which were provided at our request, one day at
Mr Mitchelson's, where we dined – The first put me in mind of
the history of Congo, in which I had read of negroes' heads sold
publickly in the markets; the last, being a mess of minced lights,
livers, suet, oat-meal, onions, and pepper, inclosed in a sheep's
stomach, had a very sudden effect upon mine, and the delicate
Mrs Tabby changed colour; when the cause of our disgust was
instantaneously removed at the nod of our entertainer. The
Scots, in general, are attached to this composition, with a sort
of national fondness.

Irish Stew

From *Three Men in a Boat, 1889* | Jerome K. Jerome (1859–1927)

It was still early when we got settled, and George said that, as we had plenty of time, it would be a splendid opportunity to try a good, slap-up supper. He said he would show us what could be done up the river in the way of cooking, and suggested that, with the vegetables and the remains of the cold beef and general odds and ends, we should make an Irish stew.

. . . .

George stirred it all up, and then he said that there seemed to be a lot of room to spare, so we overhauled both the hampers, and picked out all the odds and ends and the remnants, and added them to the stew. There were half a pork pie and a bit of cold boiled bacon left, and we put them in. Then George found half a tin of potted salmon, and he emptied that into the pot.

He said that was the advantage of Irish stew: you got rid of such a lot of things. I fished out a couple of eggs that had got cracked, and put those in. George said they would thicken the gravy.

I forget the other ingredients, but I know nothing was wasted; and I remember that, towards the end, Montmorency, who had evinced great interest in the proceedings throughout, strolled away with an earnest and thoughtful air, reappearing, a few minutes afterwards, with a dead water-rat in his mouth, which he evidently wished to present as his contribution to the dinner; whether in a sarcastic spirit, or with a genuine desire to assist, I cannot say.

We had a discussion as to whether the rat should go in or not. Harris said that he thought it would be all right, mixed up with the other things, and that every little helped; but George stood up for precedent. He said he had never heard of water-rats in Irish stew, and he would rather be on the safe side, and not try experiments. Harris said:

If you never try a new thing, how can you tell what it's like? It's men such as you that hamper the world's progress. Think of the man who first tried German sausage!'

It was a great success, that Irish stew. I don't think I ever enjoyed a meal more. There was something so fresh and piquant about it. One's palate gets so tired of the old hackneyed things: here was a dish with a new flavour, with a taste like nothing else on earth.

And it was nourishing, too. As George said, there was good stuff in it. The peas and potatoes might have been a bit softer, but we all had good teeth, so that did not matter much: and as for the gravy, it was a poem – a little too rich, perhaps, for a weak stomach, but nutritious.

9 August

Bœuf en Daube

From *To the Lighthouse, 1927* | Virginia Woolf (1882–1941)

She wished the dinner to be particularly nice, since William Bankes had at last consented to dine with them; and they were having Mildred's masterpiece – Bœuf en Daube. Everything depended upon things being served up to the precise moment they were ready. The beef, the bayleaf, and the wine – all must be done to a turn. To keep it waiting was out of the question.

. . . .

An exquisite scent of olives and oil and juice rose from the great brown dish as Marthe, with a little flourish, took the cover off. The cook had spent three days over that dish. And she must take great care, Mrs. Ramsay thought, diving into the soft mass, to choose a specially tender piece for William Bankes. And she peered into the dish, with its shiny walls and its confusion of savoury brown and yellow meats and its bay leaves and its wine, and thought: This will celebrate the occasion.

The Hummus Wars

From *Jerusalem, 2012* | Yotam Ottolenghi (1968–) and Sami Tamimi (1968–)

A hummusia is a simple eatery specializing almost only in hummus, which is normally open for breakfast and until late afternoon. It is, like the English chippy, a savoured local treasure. Yet, typically, it carries with is much stronger sentiments. The hummusia fetish is so powerful that even the best of friends may easily turn against each other if they suddenly find themselves on opposite hummus camps.

. . . .

Abu Shukri was for years considered one of the best hummusia in the country, rivalled only by the famous Abu Hassan in Jaffa or Said's in Acre (or Akko). One day, across the unpaved dirt road, another hummusia opened, with a little sign hanging over the door saying 'We moved here. This is the real Abu Shukri.' The newcomer, believe it or not, was Abu Shukri's son-in-law, an ex-waiter. The outrage! The next day the old restaurant hung a sign on its door: 'We didn't move anywhere. This is the real Abu Shukri.' A large banner appeared across the road not long afterwards: 'The real real, one and only, Abu Shukri.' You can probably imagine what followed. In the end, after years of fierce rivalry and many confused diners mistaking one Abu Shukri for the other, a big food corporation selling packed hummus in supermarket decided to run a TV campaign to promote its own brand. It culminated in a big reconciliation event between the two Abu Shukris and was labelled 'The End of Hummus Wars'.

The Tripe and Pea Shop

From *The Road to Wigan Pier, 1937* | George Orwell (1903–1950)

The shop was a narrow, cold sort of room. On the outside of the window a few white letters, relics of ancient chocolate advertisements, were scattered like stars. Inside there was a slab upon which lay the great white folds of tripe, and the grey flocculent stuff known as 'black tripe', and the ghostly translucent feet of pigs, ready boiled. It was the ordinary 'tripe and pea' shop, and not much else was stocked except bread, cigarettes, and tinned stuff. 'Teas' were advertised in the window, but if a customer demanded a cup of tea he was usually put off with excuses. Mr Brooker, though out of work for two years, was a miner by trade, but he and his wife had been keeping shops of various kinds as a side-line all their lives. At one time they had had a pub, but they had lost their licence for allowing gambling on the premises. I doubt whether any of their businesses had ever paid; they were the kind of people who run a business chiefly in order to have something to grumble about. Mr Brooker was a dark, small-boned, sour, Irish-looking man, and astonishingly dirty. I don't think I ever once saw his hands clean. As Mrs Brooker was now an invalid he prepared most of the food, and like all people with permanently dirty hands he had a peculiarly intimate, lingering manner of handling things. If he gave you a slice of bread-and-butter there was always a black thumb-print on it. Even in the early morning when he descended into the mysterious den behind Mrs Brooker's sofa and fished out the tripe, his hands were already black. I heard dreadful stories from the other lodgers about the place where the tripe was kept. Black-beetles were said to swarm there. I do not know how often fresh consignments of tripe were ordered, but it was at long intervals, for Mrs Brooker used to date events by it. 'Let me see now, I've had in three lots of froze (frozen tripe) since that happened,' etc. etc. We lodgers were never given tripe to eat. At the time I imagined that this was because tripe was too expensive; I have since thought that it was merely because we knew too much about it. The Brookers never ate tripe themselves, I noticed.

Undue Significance

Emily Dickinson (1830–1886)

Undue Significance a starving man attaches
To Food –
Far off – He sighs – and therefore – Hopeless –
And therefore – Good –
Partaken – it relieves – indeed –
But proves us
That Spices fly
In the Receipt – It was the Distance –
Was Savory –

The Christmas Seasons

From *Elizabeth David's Christmas, 2003*

Elizabeth David (1913–1992)

Christmas comes but once a year. Don't ever say that to a cookery journalist. Cookery journalists know different. For them three times a year would be nearer the mark. First, around mid-August, when they must start work on the recipes, at any rate if they contribute regularly to a glossy monthly. There'll probably be colour photographs to cook for and supervise as well. The next round comes about the end of September when the article has to be written and something original – well, anyway different from last year – dredged up in the way of advice about the turkey and the leftovers. The third time it actually is Christmas, when it's all cooked for real, although not without notes being made for next year's stint. In between the delivery of the monthly article there will almost certainly be another couple of Christmas pieces to write, for a weekly, a wine merchant's newsletter, a Sunday, a daily.

Definition of Man

From *The Journal of a Tour to the Hebrides, 1785*

James Boswell (1740–1795)

Sunday 15th August

An ancient philosopher said, Man was a 'two-legged animal without feathers', upon which his rival Sage had a Cock plucked bare, and set him down in the school before all the disciples, as a 'Philosophick Man'. Dr Franklin said, man was 'a tool-making animal', which is very well; for no animal but man makes a thing, by means of which he can make another thing. But this applies to very few of the species. My definition of *Man* is, 'a Cooking Animal'. The beasts have memory, judgment and all the faculties and passions of our mind, in a certain degree; but no beast is a cook. The trick of the monkey using the cat's paw to roast a chestnut is only a piece of shrewd malice in that *turpissima bestia*, which humbles us so sadly by its similarity to us. Man alone can dress a good dish; and every man whatever is more or less a cook, in seasoning what he himself eats.

Friendly Terms

From *The Notebooks of Samuel Butler, 1912*

Samuel Butler (1835–1902)

Man is the only animal that can remain on friendly terms with the victims he intends to eat until he eats them.

16 August

Ginger Pop

From *Plain Cookery for the Working Classes, 1852*

Charles Elmé Francatelli (1805–1876)

Put a *very clean* pot containing a gallon of water to boil on the fire, and as soon as it begins to boil, add twelve ounces of brown sugar, and one ounce of bruised ginger, and two ounces of cream of tartar; stir well together; pour the whole into an earthen pan, cover it over with a cloth, and let the mash remain in this state until it has become quite cold; then stir in half a gill of fresh yeast; stir all well together until thoroughly mixed, cover the pan over with a cloth, and leave the ginger-beer in a cool place to work up; this will take from six to eight hours; the scum which has risen to the top must then be carefully removed with a spoon without disturbing the brightness of the beer; it is then to be carefully poured off bright into a jug with a spout, to enable you easily to pour it into the bottles. These must be immediately corked down tight, tied across the corks with string, and put away, lying down in the cellar. The ginger-pop will be fit to drink in about four days after it has been bottled.

Dogs Don't Like Ginger-beer

From *Five Run Away Together, 1944* | Enid Blyton (1897–1968)

Timmy was thirsty. He sat with his tongue hanging out, wishing that George would give him a drink. He didn't like ginger-beer.

George eyed him lazily.

'Oh Timmy – are you thirsty?' she said. 'Oh dear, I feel as if I really can't get up! You'll have to wait a few minutes, then I'll go to the boat and empty out some water for you.'

But Timmy couldn't wait. He went off to some nearby rocks, which were out of reach of the sea. In a hole in one of them he found some rain-water, and he lapped it up eagerly. The children heard him lapping it, and laughed.

'Isn't Timmy clever?' murmured Anne. 'I should never have thought of that.'

Voluptuous Teas

From *Miss Mapp, 1922* | E. F. Benson (1867–1940)

Tea, followed by a bridge-party, was, in summer, the chief
manifestation of the spirit of hospitality in Tilling. Mrs. Poppit, it
is true, had attempted to do something in the way of dinner-parties,
but though she was at liberty to give as many dinner-parties as she
pleased, nobody else had followed her ostentatious example. Dinner-
parties entailed a higher scale of living; Miss Mapp, for one, had
accurately counted the cost of having three hungry people to dinner,
and found that one such dinner-party was not nearly compensated
for, in the way of expense, by being invited to three subsequent
dinner-parties by your guests. Voluptuous teas were the rule,
after which you really wanted no more than little bits of things,
a cup of soup, a slice of cold tart, or a dished-up piece of fish and
some toasted cheese.

19 August

273

Hospitality

From *Wild Wales, 1862* | George Borrow (1803–1881)

'Pray, gentleman, walk in!' said the miller; 'we are going to have our afternoon's meal, and shall be rejoiced if you will join us.'

'Yes, do, gentleman,' said the miller's wife, for such the good woman was; 'and many a welcome shall you have.'

I hesitated, and was about to excuse myself.

'Don't refuse, gentleman!' said both, 'surely you are not too proud to sit down with us?'

'I am afraid I shall only cause you trouble,' said I.

'Dim blinder, no trouble,' exclaimed both at once; 'pray do walk in!'

I entered the house, and the kitchen, parlour, or whatever it was, a nice little room with a slate floor. They made me sit down at a table by the window, which was already laid for a meal. There was a clean cloth upon it, a tea-pot, cups and saucers, a large plate of bread-and-butter, and a plate, on which were a few very thin slices of brown, watery cheese.

My good friends took their seats, the wife poured out tea for the stranger and her husband, helped us both to bread-and-butter and the watery cheese, then took care of herself. Before, however, I could taste the tea, the wife, seeming to recollect herself, started up, and hurrying to a cupboard, produced a basin full of snow-white lump sugar, and taking the spoon out of my hand, placed two of the largest lumps in my cup, though she helped neither her husband nor herself; the sugar-basin being probably only kept for grand occasions.

My eyes filled with tears; for in the whole course of my life I had never experienced so much genuine hospitality.

Ash Cake

From *My Bondage and My Freedom*, 1855

Frederick Douglass (1818–1895)

The dinner of the slaves consisted of a huge piece of ash cake, and a small piece of pork, or two salt herrings. Not having ovens, nor any suitable cooking utensils, the slaves mixed their meal with a little water, to such thickness that a spoon would stand erect in it; and, after the wood had burned away to coals and ashes, they would place the dough between oak leaves and lay it carefully in the ashes, completely covering it; hence, the bread is called ash cake. The surface of this peculiar bread is covered with ashes, to the depth of a sixteenth part of an inch, and the ashes, certainly, do not make it very grateful to the teeth, nor render it very palatable. The bran, or coarse part of the meal, is baked with the fine, and bright scales run through the bread. This bread, with its ashes and bran, would disgust and choke a northern man, but it is quite liked by the slaves. They eat it with avidity, and are more concerned about the quantity than about the quality. They are far too scantily provided for, and are worked too steadily, to be much concerned for the quality of their food.

The Diet

From *Letter on Corpulence, 1863* | William Banting (1797–1878)

For breakfast, I take four or five ounces of beef, mutton, kidneys, broiled fish, bacon, or cold meat of any kind except pork; a large cup of tea (without milk or sugar), a little biscuit, or one ounce of dry toast.

For dinner, Five or six ounces of any fish except salmon, any meat except pork, any vegetable except potato, one ounce of dry toast, fruit out of a pudding, any kind of poultry or game, and two or three glasses of good claret, sherry, or Madeira – Champagne, Port and Beer forbidden.

For tea, Two or three ounces of fruit, a rusk or two, and a cup of tea without milk or sugar.

For supper, Three or four ounces of meat or fish, similar to dinner, with a glass or two of claret.

For nightcap, if required, a tumbler of grog – (gin, whiskey, or brandy, without sugar) – or a glass or two of claret or sherry.

[In August 1862 William Banting weighed 202 lbs., exactly one year later, he weighed 156 lbs., a loss of 46 lbs.]

Figs

D. H. Lawrence (1885–1930)

Lines 1–9

The proper way to eat a fig, in society,

Is to split it in four, holding it by the stump,

And open it, so that it is a glittering, rosy, moist, honied, heavy
petalled four-petalled flower.

Then you throw away the skin

Which is just like a four-sepalled calyx,

After you have taken off the blossom with your lips.

But the vulgar way

Is just to put your mouth to the crack, and take out the flesh in
one bite.

Every fruit has its secret.

San Gervasio.

Strong Mead

From *The Closet of the Eminently Learned Sir Kenelme Digbie Kt. Opened, 1669* | Sir Kenelm Digby (1603–1665)

Take one Measure of honey, and dissolve it in four of water, beating it long up and down with clean Woodden ladels. The next day boil it gently, scumming it all the while till no more scum riseth; and if you will clarifie the Liquor with a few beaten whites of Eggs, it will be the clearer. The rule of it's being boiled enough is, when it yieldeth no more scum, and beareth an Egge, so that the breadth of a groat is out of the water. Then pour it out of the Kettle into woodden vessels, and let it remain there till it be almost cold. Then Tun it into a vessel, where Sack hath been.

Drinking Song

J. K. Stephen (1859–1892)

There are people, I know, to be found,
 Who say, and apparently think,
That sorrow and care may be drowned
 By a timely consumption of drink.

Does not man, these enthusiasts ask,
 Most nearly approach the divine,
When engaged in the soul-stirring task
 Of filling his body with wine?

Have not beggars been frequently known,
 When satisfied, soaked, and replete,
To imagine their bench was a throne
 And the civilised world at their feet?

Lord Byron has finely described
 The remarkably soothing effect
Of liquor, profusely imbibed,
 On a soul that is shattered and wrecked.

In short, if your body or mind
 Or your soul or your purse come to grief,
You need only get drunk, and you'll find
 Complete and immediate relief.

For myself, I have managed to do
 Without having recourse to this plan,
So I can't write a poem for you,
 And you'd better get someone who can.

Dr Henderson

From *Nose to Tail Eating, 1999* | Fergus Henderson (1963–)

Here is my cure for any overindulgence, taught to me by my
wise father.

2 parts Fernet Branca
1 part Crème de Menthe
Ice

Mix together and drink. Do not be put off by the colour.

Be careful, this is so effective you can find yourself turning to its
miraculous powers with increasing regularity. Do not let the cure
become the cause.

26 August

An Extemporised Supper

From *The Diary of a Nobody, 1892*

George Grossmith (1847–1912) and Weedon Grossmith (1854–1919)

August 27

Carrie prepared a little extemporised supper, consisting of the
remainder of the cold joint, a small piece of salmon (which I was to
refuse, in case there was not enough to go round), and a blanc-mange
and custards. There was also a decanter of port and some jam puffs
on the sideboard.

Dinner-giving Snobs

From *The Book of Snobs, 1848* |

William Makepeace Thackeray (1811–1863)

Suppose you, in the middle rank of life, accustomed to Mutton, roast on Tuesday, cold on Wednesday, hashed on Thursday, &c., with small means and a small establishment, choose to waste the former and set the latter topsy-turvy by giving entertainments unnaturally costly – you come into the Dinner-giving Snob class at once. Suppose you get in cheap-made dishes from the pastrycook's, and hire a couple of greengrocers, or carpet-beaters, to figure as footmen, dismissing honest Molly, who waits on common days, and bedizening your table (ordinarily ornamented with willow-pattern crockery) with twopenny-halfpenny Birmingham plate. Suppose you pretend to be richer and grander than you ought to be – you are a Dinner-giving Snob. And oh, I tremble to think how many and many a one will read this!

A man who entertains in this way – and, alas, how few do not! – is like a fellow who would borrow his neighbour's coat to make a show in, or a lady who flaunts in the diamonds from next door – a humbug, in a word, and amongst the Snobs he must be set down.

Huckleberries on Fair Haven Hill

From *Walden, 1854* | Henry David Thoreau (1817–1862)

The fruits do not yield their true flavor to the purchaser of them, nor to him who raises them for the market. There is but one way to obtain it, yet few take that way. If you would know the flavor of huckleberries, ask the cow-boy or the partridge. It is a vulgar error to suppose that you have tasted huckleberries who never plucked them. A huckleberry never reaches Boston; they have not been known there since they grew on her three hills. The ambrosial and essential part of the fruit is lost with the bloom which is rubbed off in the market cart, and they become mere provender. As long as Eternal Justice reigns, not one innocent huckleberry can be transported thither from the country's hills.

29 August

British Picnics

From *Picnic, 1981* | Claudia Roden (1936–)

Despite our grey and drizzly weather, picnics have become a British institution. Forever endearing is the romantic nostalgia and sublime recklessness with which people continue to indulge in the national passion at great social events like Henley Regatta and Glyndebourne, the Chelsea Flower Show, Goodwood and Ascot and on Epsom Downs on Derby Day. Race meetings, agricultural shows, sports days and regattas see thousands of enthusiasts eating their lunch in the rain and snow. City parks on chilly spring days are full of office workers at lunch-time. Glorious weather or not, bank holidays bring crowds to Hampstead Heath, and every summer scores of people set off with hampers and picnic baskets to the sea, the woods or the fields.

. . . .

It does require stoicism to defy fate and bring out knives and forks at the risk of being rained and blown upon. But it is also true that the gastronomic rigours of British hotels and restaurants are usually worse than those of the British climate, and there seems to be a particular, grim, English pleasure in a cold, wet, uncomfortable picnic. Jane Grigson has remarked that often, the success of a picnic depends on disaster. Judging by the abundance of catastrophes described with glee in English diaries and fiction, it must be so. Stories abound of rain and umbrellas blown away, of wet, wasp-infested fields, of pots fallen in the fire, and soggy bread.

Saint's Days

From *Perfume from Provence, 1935* | Winifred Fortescue (1888–1951)

We ran out of butter to-day. Emilia, my little *bonne*, confesses to me that she has a small hole in her head through which things necessary to remember sometimes escape. Very inconvenient that little hole can be. Needless to say, to-day is a *jour de fête*. It always seems to be a Saint's Day when we run out of butter, or milk, or other vital things, and then, of course, all the shops are shut, and the only hope left to us is that some kindly peasant neighbour, remembering the holiday (for to him it means a 'bean-feast') may have laid in a double store of provisions to entertain his friends.

One day I shall learn which of the saints are important enough to paralyse the commercial activities of the neighbouring town.

31 August

SEPTEMBER

The Table Seemed to Groan

Trimalchio's Chef

From *The Satyricon, c.* AD 63–65 | Petronius (AD 27–66)

Translated by William Burnaby (1673–1706)

Supplements of this translation were later proved to be spurious.

1 September

Nor had there ever been an end of this trumpery, had not that last service of blackbirds, baked in a good pie-crust with raisins and chestnuts, been brought up, and after them quince-peaches, so stuck with prickles, that they look'd like hedgehogs: Yet this might have been born with, if the next dish had not been such, that we had rather starved than touch'd it: For when it was set upon the table, and as we thought, a fat goose, with fishes and all kind of fowl around it, whatever you see here, said Trimalchio is all made of the same substance.

I, like a cunning cur, straight apprehended what it might be; and turning to Agamemnon, 'I marvel,' said I, 'whether they be all mash'd together or made of loam; for in a Saturnal at Rome, myself saw the like imaginary shew of a supper.'

Nor had I scarce said it, when – quoth Trimalchio, 'Let me so grow in estate, not bulk, as my cook made all of this out of one hog; there is not an exellenter fellow than himself; he shall, if he please, make ye a pol of ling of a sows tripe; a wood-culver of fat bacon; a turtle of a spring of pork; and a hen of a collar of brawn; and therefore of my own fancy, I gave him a proper name to him, for he is called Dædalus: And because he understands his business, I had chopping knives of the best steel brought him from Rome'; and with that, calling for them, he turn'd them over, and admiring them, offered us the liberty of trying their edge on his cheek.

Sing a Song of Sixpence

Anon

Sing a song of sixpence,
    A pocket full of rye;
Four and twenty blackbirds,
    Baked in a pie.

When the pie was opened,
    The birds began to sing;
Was not that a dainty dish,
    To set before the king?

The king was in the counting-house,
    Counting out his money;
The queen was in the parlour,
    Eating bread and honey,

The maid was in the garden,
    Hanging out the clothes,
Along came a blackbird,
    And snipped off her nose.

Frogs and Birds

From *The Cooks and Confectioners Dictionary, 1723*

John Nott (late 17th–early 18th century)

Some divertissements:

The two great Pyes still remaining untouch'd, some or other will have the Curiosity to see what's in them, and, lifting off the Lid of one Pye, out jump the Frogs; this makes the Ladies skip and scamper, and lifting up the Lid of the other, out fly the Birds, which will naturally fly at the Light, and so put out the Candles, and so with the leaping of the Frogs below, and flying of the Birds above, it will cause a surprising and diverting Hurly-Burley amongst the Guests in the Dark; after which, the Candles being lighted, the Banquet is brought in, the Musick sounds, and the Particular of each Person's Surprize and Adventures, furnish Matter for diverting Discourse.

Dining with the Bishop

From *The Diary of a Country Parson, 1783*

James Woodforde (1740–1803)

Sep. 4

About 1. o'clock Mr. and Mrs. Custance called here in their Coach
and took me with them to Norwich to dine with the Bishop. I was
dressed in a Gown and Cassock and Scarf. We got to the Palace
abt. 3. o'clock, and there dined and spent the Afternoon with his
Lordship Dr. Bagot, and his Lady Mrs. Bagot, whose Name before
Marriage was Miss Hay, the two Miss Hay's her Sisters, two Mr.
Hay's her Brothers, a Mr. Gooch the Bishop's Chaplain, Dr. Brook
of Yarmouth, Mr. Buxton of Easton, and his Nephew the Revd.
Mr. Buxton, Mr. Du Quesne, Mr. Priest of Reepham, and 5 strange
Clergymen.

There were 20 of us at the Table and a very elegant Dinner the
Bishop gave us. We had 2 Courses of 20 Dishes each Course, and a
Desert after of 20 Dishes. Madeira, red and white Wines. The first
Course amongst many other things were 2 Dishes of prodigious fine
stewed Carp and Tench, and a fine Haunch of Venison. Amongst
the second Course a fine Turkey Poult, Partridges, Pidgeons and
Sweatmeats. Desert – amongst other things, Mulberries, Melon,
Currants, Peaches, Nectarines and Grapes.

The Highest Pretension

From *Lothair, 1870* | Benjamin Disraeli (1804–1881)

The repast was sumptuous; Lothair thought the dinner would never
end, there were so many dishes, and apparently all of the highest
pretension. But if his simple tastes had permitted him to take an
interest in these details, which, they did not, he would have been
assisted by a gorgeous menu of gold and white typography, that was
by the side of each guest. The table seemed literally to groan under
vases and gigantic flagons, and, in its midst, rose a mountain of
silver, on which apparently all the cardinal virtues, several of the
pagan deities, and Britannia herself, illustrated with many lights
a glowing inscription, which described the fervent feelings of a
grateful client.

5 September

The Right Spirit

From *Anecdotes of Destiny: Babette's Feast, 1958*

Isak Dinesen / Karen Blixen (1885–1962)

The dinner at which the guests had vowed not to mention the food:

Most often the people in Berlevaag during the course of a good
meal would come to feel a little heavy. Tonight it was not so. The
convives grew lighter in weight and lighter of heart the more they ate
and drank. They no longer needed to remind themselves of their vow.
It was, they realized, when man has not only altogether forgotten
but has firmly renounced all ideas of food and drink that he eats and
drinks in the right spirit.

6 September

How to Eat Grapes

From *The Notebooks of Samuel Butler, 1912* |

Samuel Butler (1835–1902)

Always eat grapes downwards – that is, always eat the best grape first; in this way there will be none better left on the bunch, and each grape will seem good down to the last. If you eat the other way, you will not have a good grape in the lot. Besides, you will be tempting Providence to kill you before you come to the best. This is why autumn seems better than spring: in the autumn we are eating our days downwards, in the spring each day still seems 'Very bad.' People should live on this principle more than they do, but they do live on it a good deal; from the age of, say, fifty we eat our days downwards.

7 September

Grapes

From *Robinson Crusoe, 1719* | Daniel Defoe (1660–1731)

The next day, the 16th, I went up the same way again, and after
going something further than I had gone the day before, I found the
brook, and the savannas cease, and the country began to become
more woody than before. In this part I found different fruits, and
particularly I found melons upon the ground in great abundance,
and grapes upon the trees; the vines had spread indeed over the
trees, and the clusters of grapes were just now in their prime, very
ripe and rich. This was a surprising discovery, and I was exceeding
glad of them; but I was warned by my experience to eat sparingly of
them, remembering that, when I was ashore in Barbary, the eating
of grapes killed several of our Englishmen, who were slaves there, by
throwing them into fluxes and fevers. But I found an excellent use for
these grapes, and that was to cure or dry them in the sun, and keep
them as dried grapes or raisins are kept; which I thought would be,
as indeed they were, wholesome and agreeable to eat when no grapes
might be to be had.

Rationing

From *Feast Days, 1990* | Jennifer Paterson (1928–1999)

The Spectator, 1986

I might as well jump on the bandwagon of this 50th anniversary of the commencement of the late unpleasantness with everybody else. I recall the air raid sirens going off almost immediately war had been announced so we all sat under the stairwell waiting to be gassed at once and were rather amazed when nothing happened. The next day my mother bought several tins of soft herring roes and jars of olives as emergency food; we ate them within a week and that was that, nothing was ever stored again. But we did have a great bargaining power: tea. None of us drank it, having been brought up on sweet black coffee. Tea became gold-dust and coffee was never rationed.

Rations – an allowance of ¼ lb of butter, ¼ lb of bacon and ¾ lb of sugar, reduced to ½ lb later on, red meat to the equivalent of a couple of chops a week, though offal was never rationed if you could find it, likewise poultry and fish; very little cheese unless you chose to register as a vegetarian. All this added up to a far healthier Britain, so we are told.

Free concentrated orange juice and cod-liver oil for the kiddies, who didn't like it, so the juice was often used to enlivened gin which was itself pretty scarce, as were all such helpful beverages. We used to make mayonnaise with powdered egg, liquid paraffin and vinegar. We thought it marvellous at the time; can you imagine anything more revolting?

The Size

George Herbert (1593–1633)

Verses 1–3

     Content thee, greedy heart.
Modest and moderate joys to those, that have
Title to more hereafter when they part,
         Are passing brave.
  Let th' upper springs into the low
  Descend and fall, and thou dost flow.

     What though some have a fraught
Of cloves and nutmegs, and in cinnamon sail;
If thou hast wherewithall to spice a draught,
         When griefs prevail;
  And for the future time art heir
  To th' Isle of spices, is't not fair?

     To be in both worlds full
Is more than God was, who was hungry here.
Wouldst thou his laws of fasting disannul?
         Enact good cheer?
  Lay out thy joy, yet hope to save it?
  Wouldst thou both eat thy cake, and have it?

Bread

From *De Agricultura / On Farming, c. 160 BC* | Marcus Porcius Cato
(234–149 BC)

Translated by Henry David Thoreau (1817–1862)

'Panem depsticium sic facito. Manus mortariumque bene lavato.
Farinam in mortarium indito, aquæ paulatim addito, subigitoque
pulchre. Ubi bene subegeris, defingito, coquitoque sub testu.'

Which I take to mean:
Make kneaded bread thus: Wash your hands and trough well. Put the
meal into the trough, add water gradually, and knead it thoroughly.
When you have kneaded it well, mould it, and bake it under a cover,
that is, in a baking-kettle.
Not a word about leaven.

11 September

Clap Bread

From *Through England on a Side-Saddle in the Time of William and Mary, 1888* | Celia Fiennes (1662–1741)

Lake Wiandermer

Here it was I saw y oat Clap bread made. They mix their flour with water, so soft as to rowle it in their hands into a ball, and then they have a board made round and something hollow in the middle riseing by degrees all round to the Edge a little higher, but so little as one would take it to be only a board warp'd, this is to Cast out the Cake thinn and so they Clap it round and drive it to y Edge in a Due proportion till drove as thinn as a paper and still they Clap it and drive it round, and then they have a plaite of iron same size with their Clap board, and so shove off the Cake on it and so set it on Coales and bake it; when Enough on one side they slide it off and put the other side; if their iron plaite is smooth and they take Care their Coales or Embers are not too hot but just to make it Looke yellow, it will bake and be as Crisp and pleasant to Eate as any thing you Can imagine, but as we say of all sorts of bread there is a vast deal of difference in what is housewifely made and what is ill made, so this if its well mixed and Rowled up and but a little flour on the outside which will drye on and make it mealy is a very good sort of food. This is the sort of bread they use in all these Countrys, and in Scotland they breake into their milk or broth or Else sup that up and bite off their bread between while they spread butter on it and Eate it with their meate.

Lunch

From *Tender at the Bone, 1998* | Ruth Reichl (1948–)

Monsieur du Croix sat at the head of the long table:

'*Asseyez-vous,*' he commanded, picking up a ladle by his plate and dipping it into a terrine of soup. A butler stood before him holding out a bowl, and he slowly splashed it full of a thick orange liquid. Then the butler walked solemnly round the table, distributing bowls by age and rank. The soup was fragrant and steamed invitingly. I sat, tantalized, waiting for Madame du Croix to lift her spoon.

Finally she did. I dipped my own spoon into the thick liquid and brought it to my mouth. With the first sip I knew that I had never really eaten before. The initial taste was pure carrot, followed by cream, butter, a bit of nutmeg. I swallowed and my whole mouth and throat filled with the echo of a rich chicken stock. I took another bite and it began all over again. I ate as if in a dream.

Consommé Viveur

From *Venus in the Kitchen: or Love's Cookery Book, 1952*

Norman Douglas (1868–1952)

Take some good strong consommé and bring it to a lively boil. Throw in a handful or two of fresh celery, stalks, leaves and all, and cook, uncovered, for about five minutes.

Fish out the celery, cloud the consommé with a teaspoonful of cream and serve at once, sprinkled with a little chopped chervil.

Very stimulating indeed.

14 September

Breakfast in Bed

From *Elizabeth and Her German Garden, 1898*

Elizabeth von Arnim (1866–1941)

September 15th

No friendship can stand the breakfast test, and here, in the
country, we invariably think it our duty to appear at breakfast.
Civilisation has done away with curl-papers, yet at that hour the
soul of the Hausfrau is as tightly screwed up in them as was ever her
grandmother's hair; and though my body comes down mechanically,
having been trained that way by punctual parents, my soul never
thinks of beginning to wake up for other people till lunch-time, and
never does so completely till it has been taken out of doors and aired
in the sunshine. Who can begin conventional amiability the first
thing in the morning? It is the hour of savage instincts and natural
tendencies; it is the triumph of the Disagreeable and the Cross. I am
convinced that the Muses and the Graces never thought of having
breakfast anywhere but in bed.

Drinking Ava

From *Polynesian Researches: Hawaii, 1832*

William Ellis (1794–1872)

Soon after we had entered Miomioi's house, a salt flying-fish was broiled for supper. A large copper broiler was also brought out, and tea was made with some dried mint, which, he said, he had procured many months before from ships at Towaihae. He supped at the same time, but, instead of drinking tea, took a large cocoa-nut shell full of *ava*. If an opinion of its taste might be formed by the distortion of his countenance after taking it, it must be a most nauseous dose. There seemed to be about half a pint of it in the cup; its colour was like thick dirty calcareous water. As he took it, a man stood by his side with a calabash of fresh water, and the moment he had swallowed the intoxicating dose, he seized the calabash, and drank a hearty draught of water, to remove the unpleasant taste and burning effect of the ava.

The *ava* has been used for the purpose of inebriation by most of the South Sea Islanders, and is prepared from the roots and stalks of a species of pepper plant, the *piper methysticum* of Forster, which is cultivated for this purpose in many of the islands, and, being a plant of slow growth, was frequently tabu'd from the common people. The water in which the ava had been macerated, was the only intoxicating liquor with which the natives were acquainted before their intercourse with foreigners, and was, comparatively speaking, but little used, and sometimes only medicinally, to cure cutaneous eruptions and prevent corpulency.

16 September

Recipe for Martini

From *Casino Royale, 1953* | Ian Fleming (1908–1964)

Bond looked carefully at the barman.

'A dry martini,' he said. 'One. In a deep champagne goblet.'

'*Oui, monsieur.*'

'Just a moment. Three measures of Gordon's, one of vodka, half a measure of Kina Lillet. Shake it very well, until it's ice-cold, then add a large thin slice of lemon peel. Got it?'

'Certainly, monsieur.' The barman seemed pleased with the idea.

'Gosh, that's certainly a drink,' said Leiter.

Bond laughed. 'When I'm … er … concentrating,' he explained, 'I never have more than one drink before dinner. But I do like that one to be large and very strong and very cold and very well-made. I hate small portions of anything, particularly when they taste bad. This drink's my own invention. I'm going to patent it when I can think of a good name.'

He watched carefully as the deep glass became frosted with the pale golden drink, slightly aerated by the bruising of the shaker. He reached for it and took a long sip.

'Excellent,' he said to the barman, 'but if you can get a vodka made with grain instead of potatoes, you will find it still better.

Potable

From *The Devil's Dictionary, 1881–1906* |

Ambrose Bierce (1842– c. 1914)

Edited by Ernest Jerome Hopkins (1887–1973)

POTABLE, n. Suitable for drinking. Water is said to be potable; indeed, some declare it our natural beverage, although even they find it palatable only when suffering from the recurrent disorder known as thirst, for which it is a medicine. Upon nothing has so great and diligent ingenuity been brought to bear in all ages and in all countries, except the most uncivilized, as upon the invention of substitutes for water. To hold that this general aversion to that liquid has no basis in the preservative instinct of the race is to be unscientific – and without science we are as the snakes and toads.

18 September

Goblin Market

Christina Rossetti (1830–1894)

Lines 1–31
Morning and evening
Maids heard the goblins cry:
'Come buy our orchard fruits,
Come buy, come buy:
Apples and quinces,
Lemons and oranges,
Plump unpecked cherries,
Melons and raspberries,
Bloom-down-cheeked peaches,
Swart-headed mulberries,
Wild free-born cranberries,
Crab-apples, dewberries,
Pine-apples, blackberries,
Apricots, strawberries;–
All ripe together
In summer weather,–
Morns that pass by,
Fair eves that fly;
Come buy, come buy:
Our grapes fresh from the vine,
Pomegranates full and fine,
Dates and sharp bullaces,
Rare pears and greengages,
Damsons and bilberries,
Taste them and try:
Currants and gooseberries,
Bright-fire-like barberries,
Figs to fill your mouth,
Citrons from the South,
Sweet to tongue and sound to eye;
Come buy, come buy.'

The Secret of the Perfect Poached Egg

From *Feast Days, 1990* | Jennifer Paterson (1928–1999)

The Spectator, 1986

I noticed in the *Times* a couple of weeks ago an article by Shona Crawford Poole (such a lovely name). She was having a terrible time trying to find a properly poached egg. Hers were served tasting of various vinegars, as it is meant to coagulate the white of the egg, but that had always been a disgusting idea and I feel for her dismay. The various other methods were very complicated, so I shall tell you the secret of the perfect poached egg, neatly formed with no whirling tentacles. James Coats, a great travelling friend of mine, discovered this method in a ship crossing the Atlantic.

Bring a frying pan of salted water to simmering point. Place an excellent egg in its shell into the water and then roll it round and round whilst intoning two Our Fathers and one Hail Mary: about half a minute. Remove egg from the water with a perforated spoon, then break into the just trembling water, cover with a lid and cook for as long as you fancy. Drain well in the spoon and serve as desired. The rolling of the egg in hot water will have set the white a tiny bit so when you crack it, it retains a nice shape.

Happy Birthday, From Hagrid

From *Harry Potter & the Philosopher's Stone, 1997*

J. K. Rowling (1965–)

'Anyway – Harry,' said the giant, turning his back on the Dursleys, 'a very happy birthday to yeh. Got summat for yeh here – I mighta sat on it at some point, but it'll taste all right.'

From inside a pocket of his black overcoat he pulled a slightly squashed box. Harry opened it with trembling fingers. Inside was a large, sticky chocolate cake with *Happy Birthday Harry* written on it in green icing.

Harry looked up at the giant. He meant to say thank you, but the words got lost in his mouth, and what he said instead was, 'Who are you?'

The giant chuckled.

21 September

Harvests

From *Perfume from Provence, 1935* | Winifred Fortescue (1888–1951)

Monsieur and I had always been childishly excited over a yield of any kind in our homes. Never shall I forget the thrill of finding the first egg from our intensive hens which we housed upon the tiny roof-garden of a small house in London during the war. At the sound of the first conceited cackle of a hen, Monsieur dashed from his garden-study where he was writing military history and tore upstairs, jostling the cook who thundered up from her basement, and the house-parlourmaid who came scudding from an upper flight, and eventually colliding with me as I shot from the drawing-room, all of us eager to be the first in the finding of the wonderful egg.

Later, in our Hampstead garden, there was the excitement of counting our cherry crop (the maximum yield was nine cherries), and our few apples, and of taking the temperature every half-hour of our precious William pear; for everyone knows it is vital to sit up all night with a William pear that is on the point of ripening lest the precious moment for picking it be lost and it become a mere potato.

The Labourer's Dyet

From *Fantasticks: serving for a perpetuall prognostication,*
1626 | Nicholas Breton (c. 1553–1626)

Harvest:
Butter, milke, and cheese, are the Labourers dyet, and a pot of good
Beere, quickens his spirit.

. . . .

Peares and Plummes now ripen apace, and being of a watry
substance, are cause of much sicknesse.

. . . .

Bucks now are in season, and Partridges are Rowen-taild, and a
good Retriver is a Spaniell worth the keeping. In sum, it is a time of
much worth, when, if God bee well pleased, the world will thrive the
better. And to conclude, this is all that I will say of it; I hold it the
Heavens Bounty, the Earths Beauty, and the Worlds Benefit.

The Permanent Larder

From *Travels with a Donkey in the Cévennes, 1879*

Robert Louis Stevenson (1850–1894)

24 September

The permanent larder was represented by cakes of chocolate and tins of Bologna sausage.

. . . .

I tied Modestine more conveniently for herself, and broke up half the black bread for her supper, reserving the other half against the morning. Then I gathered what I should want within reach, took off my wet boots and gaiters, which I wrapped in my waterproof, arranged my knapsack for a pillow under the flap of my sleeping-bag, insinuated my limbs into the interior, and buckled myself in like a *bambino*. I opened a tin of Bologna sausage and broke a cake of chocolate, and that was all I had to eat. It may sound offensive, but I ate them together, bite by bite, by way of bread and meat. All I had to wash down this revolting mixture was neat brandy: a revolting beverage in itself. But I was rare and hungry; ate well, and smoked one of the best cigarettes in my experience. Then I put a stone in my straw hat, pulled the flap of my fur cap over my neck and eyes, put my revolver ready to my hand, and snuggled well down among the sheepskins.

The School Canteen

From *Empress & Aniya, 2021* | Candice Carty-Williams (1989–)

Empress knew that in the pocket of her blazer that had been itching all morning, she had enough money for chips. Well, she had money for more, but if she bought more, it meant she wouldn't have enough to eat for the rest of the week.

'Just a portion of chips please,' Empress said quietly, as she eyed the rest of the food on offer. It all looked incredible. The mashed potato looked creamy, the crunchy greens looked fresh, the salmon looked juicy, the chicken looked plump and crispy. Empress couldn't eat dairy, but she was even ready to risk it all for the stuff covered in cheese. She was so *hungry*. Her stomach felt like it was going to eat itself.

'Nothing else, darlin'?' The canteen server asked, serving chips onto a plate. 'That's not enough to get you through the day!'

'I'm not a very big eater,' Empress lied, reaching out for the plate and putting it on the tray carefully. She just wanted the conversation to be over. She felt like people were listening and watching and she was already braced for new girl attention.

'Okay, well I've given you some extra.'

'Thanks!' Empress took the plate and practically ran over to the till to pay for her food. She wanted this whole experience over and done with. She thought about how she would have rather just bought packed lunch and eaten it in the playground, but there wasn't any food in the house so it was out of the question.

Cakes Without Eggs

The Daily Telegraph, 1939 | Tuesday 26 September

Housewives-in-council inquiries received day by day reflect the new Food Control conditions. The price of certain eggs has gone up, and yesterday's post, for example, brought many requests for recipes for eggless cakes.

Cakes of this kind are required in catering for evacuated children with hearty appetites and by housewives who want more economical cakes for ordinary use. Here are two recipes:

Eggless Cake
Butter or margarine ¼ lb, brown sugar ½ lb, flour 1 lb, sultanas ½ lb, golden syrup 2 tablespoonfuls, sour milk ½ pint, carbonate of soda 1½ teaspoonfuls.
Dissolve carbonate of soda in warm sour milk. Beat butter, sugar and golden syrup together; add dry ingredients. Mix with milk and bake for two hours in a moderate oven. The tins should be well greased.

Interesting, too, is this recipe for a Canadian war cake used in the last war, and sent in by a Virginia Water reader. It is made without butter, eggs or milk.

Two teacupfuls brown sugar, 2 teacupfuls or rather less of hot water, two tablespoons lard or margarine, 1 lb seedless raisins, 1 teaspoonful salt, cloves, cinnamon. Mixed spice may be used if preferred. Boil all ingredients together for 5 minutes after they begin to bubble. When nearly cold add 3 teacupfuls flour, 1 teaspoonful carbonate of soda dissolved in teaspoonful hot water. Bake in a slow oven 1½ to 2 hours.

Extravagance

From *How to Cook a Wolf, 1942* | M. F. K. Fisher (1908–1992)

There are very few men and women, I suspect, who cooked and
marketed their way through the last war without losing forever some
of the nonchalant extravagance of the Twenties. They will feel, until
their final days on earth, a kind of culinary caution: butter, no matter
how unlimited, is a precious substance not likely to be wasted; meats,
too, and eggs, and all the far-brought spices of the world, take on
a new significance, having once been so rare. And that is good, for
there can be no more shameful carelessness than with the food we
eat for life itself. When we exist without thought or thanksgiving we
are not men, but beasts.

27 September

Deducing Age

From *The Professor at the Breakfast Table, 1859*

Oliver Wendell Holmes Sr (1809–1894)

The crucial experiment is this – offer a bulky bun to the suspected individual just ten minutes before dinner. If this is easily accepted and devoured, the fact of youth is established.

The Green Man

From *Adam Bede, 1859* | George Eliot (1819–1880)

Hetty would need nothing at Windsor but to find Arthur:

When she had paid the fare for the last coach, she had only
a shilling; and as she got down at the sign of the Green Man in
Windsor at twelve o'clock in the middle of the seventh day, hungry
and faint, the coachman came up, and begged her to 'remember
him.' She put her hand in her pocket and took out the shilling, but
the tears came with the sense of exhaustion and the thought that
she was giving away her last means of getting food, which she really
required before she could go in search of Arthur. As she held out the
shilling, she lifted up her dark tear-filled eyes to the coachman's face
and said, 'Can you give me back sixpence?'

'No, no,' he said, gruffly, 'never mind – put the shilling up again.'

The landlord of the Green Man had stood near enough to witness
this scene, and he was a man whose abundant feeding served to keep
his good nature, as well as his person, in high condition. And that
lovely tearful face of Hetty's would have found out the sensitive fibre
in most men.

'Come, young woman, come in,' he said, 'and have a drop o'
something; you're pretty well knocked up, I can see that.'

He took her into the bar and said to his wife, 'Here, missis, take
this young woman into the parlour; she's a little overcome' – for
Hetty's tears were falling fast. They were merely hysterical tears: she
thought she had no reason for weeping now, and was vexed that she
was too weak and tired to help it. She was at Windsor at last, not far
from Arthur.

She looked with eager, hungry eyes at the bread and meat and
beer that the landlady brought her, and for some minutes she forgot
everything else in the delicious sensations of satisfying hunger and
recovering from exhaustion.

Frogs' Legs

From *Venus in the Kitchen: or Love's Cookery Book, 1952*

Norman Douglas (1868–1952)

Put three dozen frogs' legs in a saucepan with a dozen chopped mushrooms, four shallots also chopped, and two ounces of butter. Toss them on a fire for five minutes; then add a tablespoonful of flour, a little salt and pepper, grated nutmeg; and moisten with a glass of white wine and a teacupful of consommé.

Boil for ten minutes, meanwhile mix the yolks of four eggs with two tablespoons of cream. Now remove the frogs' legs and other ingredients from the fire, then add the eggs and cream, stirring continually until thoroughly mixed, and serve.

A noble aphrodisiac.

30 September

317

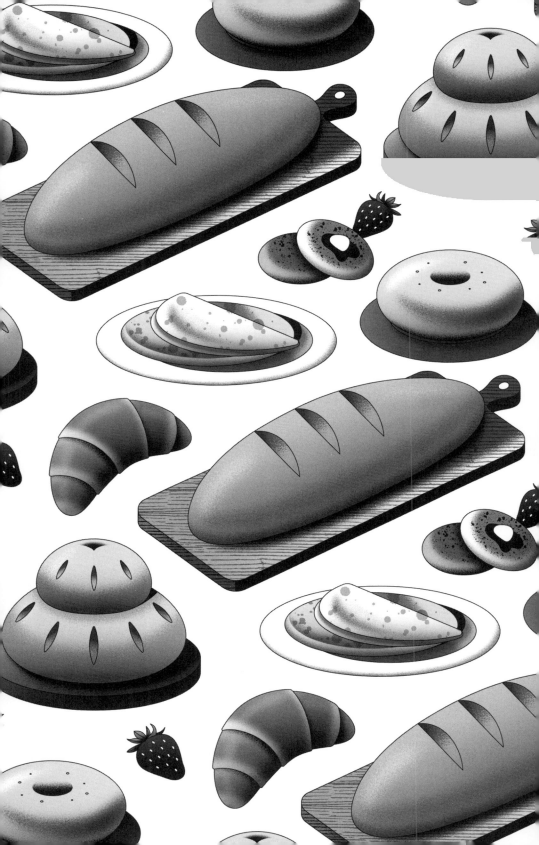

OCTOBER

The Best Repast Possible

Dinner at Oxford

From *A Room of One's Own, 1929* | Virginia Woolf (1882–1941)

Here was my soup. Dinner was being served in the great dining-hall. Far from being spring it was in fact an evening in October. Everybody was assembled in the big dining-room. Dinner was ready. Here was the soup. It was a plain gravy soup. There was nothing to stir the fancy in that. One could have seen through the transparent liquid any pattern that there might have been on the plate itself. But there was no pattern. The plate was plain. Next came beef with its attendant greens and potatoes – a homely trinity, suggesting the rumps of cattle in a muddy market, and sprouts curled and yellowed at the edge, and bargaining and cheapening, and women with string bags on Monday morning. There was no reason to complain of human nature's daily food, seeing that the supply was sufficient and coal-miners doubtless were sitting down to less. Prunes and custard followed. And if anyone complains that prunes, even when mitigated by custard, are an uncharitable vegetable (fruit they are not), stringy as a miser's heart and exuding a fluid such as might run in misers' veins who have denied themselves wine and warmth for eighty years and yet not given to the poor, he should reflect that there are people whose charity embraces even the prune. Biscuits and cheese came next, and here the water-jug was liberally passed round, for it is the nature of biscuits to be dry, and these were biscuits to the core. That was all. The meal was over. Everybody scraped their chairs back; the swing-doors swung violently to and fro; soon the hall was emptied of every sign of food and made ready no doubt for breakfast next morning.

The Two Old Bachelors

Edward Lear (1812–1888)

Two old Bachelors were living in one house;
One caught a Muffin, the other caught a Mouse.
Said he who caught the Muffin to him who caught the Mouse, –
'This happens just in time! For we've nothing in the house,
'Save a tiny slice of lemon and a teaspoonful of honey,
'And what to do for dinner – since we haven't any money?
'And what can we expect if we haven't any dinner,
'But to loose our teeth and eyelashes and keep on growing thinner?'

Said he who caught the Mouse to him who caught the Muffin, –
'We might cook this little Mouse, if we had only some Stuffin'!
'If we had but Sage and Onion we could do extremely well,
'But how to get that Stuffin' it is difficult to tell!' –

Those two old Bachelors ran quickly to the town
And asked for Sage and Onions as they wandered up and down;
They borrowed two large Onions, but no Sage was to be found
In the Shops, or in the Market, or in all the Gardens round.

But someone said, – 'A hill there is, a little to the north,
'And to its purpledicular top a narrow way leads forth; –
'And there among the rugged rocks abides an ancient Sage, –
'An earnest Man, who reads all day a most perplexing page.
'Climb up, and seize him by the toes! – all studious as he sits, –
'And pull him down, – and chop him into endless little bits!
'Then mix him with your Onion, (cut up likewise into Scraps,) –
'When your Stuffin' will be ready – and very good: perhaps.'

Those two old Bachelors without loss of time
The nearly purpledicular crags at once began to climb;
And at the top, among the rocks, all seated in a nook,
They saw that Sage, a reading of a most enormous book.

'You earnest Sage!' aloud they cried, 'your book you've read
    enough in! –
'We wish to chop you into bits to mix you into Stuffin'!' –

But that old Sage looked calmly up, and with his awful book,
At those two Bachelors' bald heads a certain aim he took –
And over crag and precipice they rolled promiscuous down, –
At once they rolled, and never stopped in lane or field or town, –
And when they reached their house, they found (besides their
    want of Stuffin',)
The Mouse had fled; – and, previously, had eaten up the Muffin.

They left their home in silence by the once convivial door.
And from that hour those Bachelors were never heard of more.

A Cook

From *The Canterbury Tales: The Prologue, 1387–1400*

Geoffrey Chaucer (c.1343–1400)

A Cook they hadde with hem for the nones,
To boille the chiknes with the mary-bones,
And poudre-marchant tart, and galingale.
Wel coude he knowe a draughte of London ale.
He coude roste, and sethe, and broille, and frye,
Maken mortreux, and wel bake a pye.
But greet harm was it, as it thoughte me,
That on his shine a mormal hadde he;
For blankmanger, that made he with the beste.

The Happiness of Mankind

From *A Handbook of Cookery for a Small House, 1923*

Jessie Conrad (1873–1936)

Preface by Joseph Conrad (1857–1924)

Preface:

Of all the books produced since the most remote ages by human talents and industry those only that treat of cooking are, from a moral point of view, above suspicion. The intention of every other piece of prose may be discussed and even mistrusted; but the purpose of a cookery book is one and unmistakable. Its object can conceivably be no other than to increase the happiness of mankind.

Sorcery

From *Chocolat, 1999* | Joanne Harris (1964–)

There is a kind of sorcery in all cooking: in the choosing of the
ingredients, the process of mixing, grating, melting, infusing and
flavouring, the recipes taken from ancient books, the traditional
utensils – the pestle and mortar with which my mother made her
incense turned to a more homely purpose, her spices and aromatics
giving up their subtleties to a baser, more sensual magic. And
it is partly the transience of it that delights me; so much loving
preparation, so much art and experience put into a pleasure which
can only last a moment, and which few will ever fully appreciate.

What Does Cookery Mean?

From *The Ethics of the Dust: Ten Lectures to Little Housewives: Home Virtues, 1866* | John Ruskin (1819–1900)

It means the knowledge of Medea, and of Circe, and of Calypso, and of Helen, and of Rebekah, and of the Queen of Sheba. It means the knowledge of all herbs, and fruits, and balms, and spices; and of all that is healing and sweet in fields and groves, and savoury in meats; it means carefulness, and inventiveness, and watchfulness, and willingness, and readiness of appliance; it means the economy of your great-grandmothers, and the science of modern chemists; it means much tasting, and no wasting; it means English thoroughness, and French art, and Arabian hospitality; and it means, in fine, that you are to be perfectly and always, 'ladies' – 'loaf-givers;' and, as you are to see, imperatively, that everybody has something pretty to put on, – so you are to see, yet more imperatively, that everybody has something nice to eat.

Kangaroo / Kanguroo

From *Le Grand Dictionnaire de la Cuisine, 1873* |

Alexandre Dumas (1802–1870)

Translated by Alan (1924–2003) and Jane (1927–2010) Davidson, 1978

Kangaroos come originally from Australia, and the surrounding islands. Essentially fruit-eaters in the wild state, kangaroos are very easy to feed when tame. They decide to eat everything which is offered to them and, it is said, even drink wine and brandy when these are given to them.

Among the mammals, the kangaroo is without question one of the animals which would be most useful and easiest to breed in Europe, either in captivity or wild. In fact, the taming of the kangaroo, as several experiments have already shown, requires practically no trouble. This is particularly true of the large kinds of kangaroo which inhabit the southern regions of Australia and Van Diemen's Land. The climate of these provinces, although temperate in general, is often very cold, and the abundant warm hair which covers the kangaroo would allow it to withstand the most rigorous winters in France without suffering too much.

The flesh of the kangaroo is excellent, especially when it has grown up wild. The rapid growth of these animals, coupled with their considerable height, produces a substantial amount of meat in very little time. In addition, the peculiar structure of these animals, which gives them back legs much larger in size than their front ones, is eminently favourable to the production of good quality meat, greatly preferable to that of the cow or sheep in that it is so much more tender than the first and nutritious than the second.

The kangaroo is timid and gentle. It is not in the least destructive, as several authors have claimed. In this respect it can be compared to the hare. It is very easy to feed.

The Dog

From *Pantropheon*, 1853 | Alexis Soyer (1810–1858)

We must beg pardon of the reader for informing him that the dog presented a very relishing dish to many nations advanced in culinary science. To them, one of these animals, young, plump, and delicately prepared, appeared excellent food.

The Greeks, that people so charming by their seductive folly, their love of the arts, their poetic civilization, and the intelligent spirit of research presiding over their dishes – the Greeks (we grieve to say it) ate dogs, and even dared to think them good: the grave Hippocrates himself – the most wise, the least gluttonous, and therefore the most impartial of their physicians – was convinced that this quadruped furnished a wholesome and, at the same time, a light food.

As to the Romans, they also liked it, and no doubt prepared it in the same manner as the hare, which they thought it resembled in taste.

However, it is but right to add, that this dish, which we will not even hear mentioned, was never favourably received by the fashionable portion of Roman society, and that the legislators of ancient gastrophagy even repulsed it with disdain.

There is every reason to believe that the people regaled themselves with a roast or boiled dog, especially once a year, at the period when they celebrated the deliverance of the Capitol from the siege of the Gauls. It is known that, at this solemnity, a goose, laid on a soft cushion, was carried in triumph, followed by an unhappy dog nailed to a cross, whose loud cries greatly amused the populace. In this manner they commemorated the signal service rendered by one animal, and the fatal negligence of the other. The Gauls scaled the Capitol while the dogs slept, and Rome had been lost if the deafening cries of the geese had not given an alarm to the garrison, who, it must be allowed, should have kept better watch.

Pears

From *The Anatomy of Dessert, 1929* | Edward Bunyard (1878–1939)

I begin with a confession. After thirty years of raising Pears I am still unfurnished with a vocabulary to describe their flavour.

I have heard it said by an Englishman that the matter is really very simple: there are but two classes of Pear – those that taste of hairwash and those that do not. No Frenchman, in his most irreverent moment, could have so insulted the queen of fruits. The Pear must be approached, as its feminine nature indicates, with discretion and reverence; it withholds its secrets from the merely hungry. Fickle and uncertain it may too often be, concealing an inward decay by a fair and smiling cheek; but when all is said, how well are we rewarded by her gracious self at its best! Forgotten are our ardours and endurances in the soft rapture of attainment.

9 October

Mr Badger's Kitchen

From *The Wind in the Willows, 1908* | Kenneth Grahame (1859–1932)

The floor was well-worn red brick, and on the wide hearth burnt a fire of logs, between two attractive chimney-corners tucked away in the wall, well out of any suspicion of draught. A couple of high-backed settles, facing each other on either side of the fire, gave further sitting accommodations for the sociably disposed. In the middle of the room stood a long table of plain boards placed on trestles, with benches down each side. At one end of it, where an arm-chair stood pushed back, were spread the remains of the Badger's plain but ample supper. Rows of spotless plates winked from the shelves of the dresser at the far end of the room, and from the rafters overhead hung hams, bundles of dried herbs, nets of onions, and baskets of eggs. It seemed a place where heroes could fitly feast after victory, where weary harvesters could line up in scores along the table and keep their Harvest Home with mirth and song, or where two or three friends of simple tastes could sit about as they pleased and eat and smoke and talk in comfort and contentment. The ruddy brick floor smiled up at the smoky ceiling; the oaken settles, shiny with long wear, exchanged cheerful glances with each other; plates on the dresser grinned at pots on the shelf, and the merry firelight flickered and played over everything without distinction.

Childhood in the Kitchen

From *Family Life, 1996* | Elisabeth Luard (1942–)

The kitchen became my refuge. Below stairs was warm and friendly with the scent of hot ovens and baking. The cook was merrily fat. Her white aprons smelt of rice-starch and blue bag. The kitchen was full of bustle and boil. No-one paid any attention to me, or even told me not to eat with my mouth open, talk with my mouth full, or scrubbed my face with a flannel as wet and rough as a shark's tongue.

There was a large oil-cloth table in the middle of the room, and it was here that all culinary activities began and ended. Sitting at it was like being in the front row of the stalls at some endless, enchanting pantomime. Sometimes, if Cook was in a good temper – and at times she had a fearful rage on her – I was allowed to take my place behind the footlights. She would swaddle me in an enormous white apron to protect my clean smocked frock, and then, wonder of wonders, she would let me roll dough and cut out biscuits, choosing my favourite scallop-edged cutter from the heavy round tin in which they were stored in magic circles, like Russian dolls.

The butter biscuits for the drawing-room tea had to be perfect: the audience must not suspect a child's hand or, so I was told, Cook would get the sack. So it was an adult task, a dangerous responsibility, and I was proud of my skill. After the upstairs biscuits had all been neatly cut out and arranged on the baking sheets, I was allowed the trimmings to make jam tarts and currant-eyed gingerbread men for the nursery.

In the kitchen, I felt useful. In the drawing-room I felt I was a nuisance. Below stairs, too, there was no shiny French-polished surfaces or little mats to protect against the rings left behind by damp saucers or dripping glasses. No-one scolded me when I put my mug of hot milk down on the table. This was the closest thing I knew to heaven, and I have been happy in the kitchen – anyone's kitchen – ever since.

An Increase in Corpulence

From *Letter on Corpulence, 1863* | William Banting (1797–1878)

I consulted an eminent surgeon, now long deceased – a kind personal
friend – who recommended increased bodily exertion before my
ordinary daily labours began, and thought rowing an excellent plan.
I had the command of a good, heavy, safe boat, lived near the river,
and adopted it for a couple of hours in the early morning. It is true
I gained muscular vigour, but with it a prodigious appetite, which
I was compelled to indulge, and consequently increased in weight,
until my kind old friend advised me to forsake the exercise.

He soon afterwards died, and, as the tendency to corpulence
remained, I consulted other high orthodox authorities (*never any
inferior adviser*), but all in vain. I have tried sea air and bathing
in various localities, with much walking exercise; taken gallons
of physic and liquor potasse, advisedly and abundantly; riding on
horseback; the waters and climate of Leamington many times, as well
as those of Cheltenham and Harrogate frequently; have lived upon
sixpence a day, so to speak, and earned it, if bodily labour may be so
construed; and have spared no trouble nor expense in consultations
with the best authorities in the land, giving each and all a fair time
for experiment, without any permanent remedy, as the evil still
gradually increased.

On the Subject of Diet

From *Rural Rides, 1830* | William Cobbett (1763–1835)

I hardly ever eat more than *twice* a day; when at home, never; and
I never, if I can well avoid it, eat any meat *later than about one or two
o'clock in the day*. I drink a little tea, or milk and water at the usual
tea-time (about 7 o'clock); I go to bed at eight, if I can; I write or
read, from about four to about eight, and then hungry as a hunter,
I go to breakfast, eating *as small a parcel* of cold meat and bread as
I can prevail upon my teeth to be satisfied with. I do just the same
at dinner time. I very rarely taste *garden-stuff* of any sort. If any
man can show me, that he has done, or can do, *more work*, bodily
and mentally united; I say nothing about *good health*, for of that the
public can know nothing; but I refer to *the work*: the public know,
they see, what I can do, and what I actually have done, and what I
do; and when any one has shown the public, that he has done, or can
do, more, then I will advise my readers attend to him, on the subject
of diet, and not to me. As to *drink*, the *less the better*; and mine is
milk and water, or *not-sour* small beer, if I can get the latter; for the
former I always can. I like the milk and water best; but I do not like
much water; and, if I drink much milk, it loads and stupefies and
makes me fat.

Buttered Toast

From *The Woman in White, 1859* | Wilkie Collins (1824–1889)

The story continued by Mrs Catherick:
My hour for tea is half-past five, and my buttered toast waits
for nobody.

Not Exactly Tea

From *The Phoenix and the Carpet, 1904* | E. Nesbit (1858–1924)

The meal of which I am speaking was not exactly tea … There was tea … But no milk could be found – so everyone had six lumps of sugar to each cup instead. The things to eat, on the other hand, were nicer than usual. The boys looked about very carefully, and found in the pantry some cold tongue, bread, butter, cheese, and part of a cold pudding – very much nicer than Cook ever made when they were at home. And in the kitchen cupboard was half a Christmassy cake, a pot of strawberry jam, and about a pound of mixed candied fruit, with soft crumbly slabs of delicious sugar in each cup of lemon, orange, or citron.

A Cross-cultural Recipe

From *Madhur Jaffrey's Cookbook: Food for Family and Friends, 1987* | Madhur Jaffrey (1933–)

I did not know until fairly recently that my grandmother was a vegetarian. You see, when she was alive and we lived together in Delhi, she sat at one end of a very long dining table and we, the little children, sat at the other end. We could all see our grandfather. He sat at the head of the table and was tall. I could see quite clearly that he drank soda water with his meals (to aid digestion, we were told) and waved his white beard about as he spoke. My grandmother, who sat to his left, was short, and somehow got lost among the protuberances of more imposing relatives. I could not see her plate, let alone what she was putting on it. Ten years ago, while visiting my oldest aunt, I found out. Whatever my grandmother was putting on her plate, I was told, it was *never* meat. I was also told that if I thought *I* was pretty clever in the kitchen, I should have seen my grandmother. Why, she *invented* 'Cauliflower with Cheese.' What sort of cheese I wondered. My grandmother was so traditionally Indian. English cheese, I was told, from the English shop. New aspects of my grandmother emerged – and a new cross-cultural recipe!

Saddle of Mutton

From *A Man of Property*, 1906 | John Galsworthy (1867–1933)

No Forsyte has given a dinner without providing a saddle of mutton. There is something in its succulent solidity which makes it suitable to people 'of a certain position.' It is nourishing and tasty; the sort of thing a man remembers eating. It has a past and a future, like a deposit paid into a bank; and it is something that can be argued about.

Each branch of the family tenaciously held to a particular locality – old Jolyon swearing by Dartmoor, James by Welsh, Swithin by Southdown, Nicholas maintaining that people might sneer, but there was nothing like New Zealand. As for Roger, the 'original' of the brothers, he had been obliged to invent a locality of his own, and with an ingenuity worthy of a man who had devised a new profession for his sons, he had discovered a shop where they sold German; on being remonstrated with, he had proved his point by producing a butcher's bill, which showed that he paid more than any of the others.

17 October

Meeting Mutton

From *Through the Looking-Glass, 1871* | Lewis Carroll (1832–1898)

There were three chairs at the head of the table; the Red and White Queens had already taken two of them, but the middle one was empty. Alice sat down in it, rather uncomfortable in the silence, and longing for some one to speak.

At last the Red Queen began. 'You've missed the soup and fish,' she said. 'Put on the joint!' And the waiters set a leg of mutton before Alice, who looked at it rather anxiously, as she had never had to carve a joint before.

'You look a little shy; let me introduce you to that leg of mutton,' said the Red Queen. 'Alice – Mutton; Mutton – Alice.' The leg of mutton got up in the dish and made a little bow to Alice; and Alice returned the bow, not knowing whether to be frightened or amused.

'May I give you a slice?' she said, taking up the knife and fork, and looking from one Queen to the other.

'Certainly not,' the Red Queen said, very decidedly: 'it isn't etiquette to cut any one you've been introduced to. Remove the joint!'

The Hen's Egg

From *How to Cook, 1998–2001* | Delia Smith (1941–)

A hen's egg is, quite simply, a work of art, a masterpiece of design and construction with, it has to be said, brilliant packaging!

Boiled Eggs and Bread and Butter

From *A Little Tour in France, 1884* | Henry James (1843–1916)

Visiting the church of Brou:

The well-fed Bressois are surely a good-natured people. I call them well-fed both on general and on particular grounds. Their province has the most savoury aroma, and I found an opportunity to test its reputation. I walked back into the town from the church (there was really nothing to be seen by the way), and as the hour of the midday breakfast had struck, directed my steps to the inn. The table d'hôte was going on, and a gracious, bustling, talkative landlady welcomed me. I had an excellent repast – the best repast possible – which consisted simply of boiled eggs and bread and butter. It was the quality of these simple ingredients that made the occasion memorable. The eggs were so good that I am ashamed to say how many of them I consumed. 'La plus belle fille du monde,' as the French proverb says, 'ne peut donner que ce qu'elle a'; and it might seem that an egg which has succeeded in being fresh has done all that can reasonably be expected of it. But there was a bloom of punctuality, so to speak, about these eggs of Bourg, as if it had been the intention of the very hens themselves that they should be promptly served. 'Nous sommes en Bresse, et le beurre n'est pas mauvais,' the landlady said with a sort of dry coquetry, as she placed this article before me. It was the poetry of butter, and I ate a pound or two of it; after which I came away with a strange mixture of impressions of late gothic sculpture and thick *tartines*.

Moonlit Apples

John Drinkwater (1882–1937)

At the top of the house the apples are laid in rows,
And the skylight lets the moonlight in, and those
Apples are deep-sea apples of green. There goes
   A cloud on the moon in the autumn night.

A mouse in the wainscot scratches, and scratches, and then
There is no sound at the top of the house of men
Or mice; and the cloud is blown, and the moon again
   Dapples the apples with deep-sea light.

They are lying in rows there, under the gloomy beams;
On the sagging floor; they gather the silver streams
Out of the moon, those moonlit apples of dreams,
   And quiet is the steep stair under.

In the corridors under there is nothing but sleep.
And stiller than ever on orchard boughs they keep
Tryst with the moon, and deep is the silence, deep
   On moon-washed apples of wonder.

Apple-dumplings

From *Essays of Elia: Grace Before Dinner, 1823*

Charles Lamb (1775–1834)

A man cannot have a pure mind who refuses apple-dumplings.

Ingredients for a Savoury Omelette

From *The Tale of Jemima Puddle-duck*, 1908 |

Beatrix Potter (1866–1943)

'I intend to give you a treat. Let us have a dinner-party all to ourselves! May I ask you to bring up some herbs from the farm-garden to make a savoury omelette? Sage and thyme, and mint and two onions, and some parsley. I will provide lard for the stuff – lard for the omelette,' said the hospitable gentleman with sandy whiskers.

Jemima Puddle-duck was a simpleton: not even the mention of sage and onions made her suspicious.

23 October

A First Taste of Duck

From *Wild Wales, 1862* | George Borrow (1803–1881)

We returned to the inn and dined. The duck was capital, and I asked John Jones if he had ever tasted a better. 'Never, sir,' said he, 'for to tell you the truth, I never tasted a duck before.' 'Rather singular,' said I. 'What, that I should not have tasted duck? Oh, sir, the singularity is, that I should now be tasting duck. Duck in Wales, sir, is not fare for poor weavers. This is the first duck I ever tasted, and though I never taste another, as I probably never shall, I may consider myself a fortunate weaver, for I can now say I have tasted duck once in my life. Few weavers in Wales are ever able to say as much.'

Definitions

From *The Devil's Dictionary, 1881–1906*

Ambrose Bierce (1842– c. 1914)

Edited by Ernest Jerome Hopkins (1887–1973)

DELIBERATION, n. The act of examining one's bread to determine which side it is buttered on.

EDIBLE, adj. Good to eat, and wholesome to digest, as a worm to a toad, a toad to a snake, a snake to a pig, a pig to a man, and a man to a worm.

EPICURE, n. An opponent of Epicurus, an abstemious philosopher who, holding that pleasure should be the chief aim of man, wasted no time in gratification from the senses.

FEAST, n. A festival. A religious celebration usually signalized by gluttony and drunkenness, frequently in honor of some holy person distinguished for abstemiousness. In the Roman Catholic Church feasts are 'movable' and 'immovable,' but the celebrants are uniformly immovable until they are full. In their earliest development these entertainments took the form of feasts for the dead; such were held by the Greeks, under the name *Nemeseia*, by the Aztecs and Peruvians, as in modern times they are popular with the Chinese; though it is believed that the ancient dead, like the modern, were light eaters. Among the many feasts of the Romans was the *Novemdiale*, which was held, according to Livy, whenever stones fell from heaven.

HOSPITALITY, n. The virtue which induces us to feed and lodge certain persons who are not in need of food and lodging.

25 October

Work at the Hotel

From *Down and Out in Paris and London, 1933*

George Orwell (1903–1950)

At a quarter to five we went back to the hotel. Till half-past six there were no orders, and we used this time to polish silver, clean out the coffee-urns, and do other odd jobs. Then the grand turmoil of the day started – the dinner hour. I wish I could be Zola for a little while, just to describe that dinner hour. The essence of the situation was that a hundred or two hundred people were demanding individually different meals of five or six courses, and that fifty or sixty people had to cook and serve them and clean up the mess afterwards; anyone with experience of catering will know what that means. And at this time when the work was doubled, the whole staff were tired out, and a number of them were drunk. I could write pages about the scene without giving a true idea of it. The chargings to and fro in the narrow passages, the collisions, the yells, the struggling with crates and trays and blocks of ice, the heat, the darkness, the furious festering quarrels which there was no time to fight out – they pass description. Anyone coming into the basement for the first time would have thought himself in a den of maniacs. It was only later, when I understood the working of the hotel, that I saw order in all this chaos.

Money Flung Out of Window

From *Paris: Book III, Spirit and Flesh, 1873* | Émile Zola (1840–1902)

Translated by Ernest A. Vizetelly (1853–1922)

They had seated themselves at table, and the repast proved a magnificent one, the service ever prompt and assiduous, an attendant being allotted to each diner. While the flowers scattered their perfumes through the room, and the plate and crystal glittered on the snowy cloth, an abundance of delicious and unexpected dishes was handed round – a sturgeon from Russia, prohibited game, truffles as big as eggs, and hothouse vegetables and fruit as full of flavour as if they had been naturally matured. It was money flung out of window, simply for the pleasure of wasting more than other people, and eating what they could not procure.

Dinner with a Duke

From *The Age of Innocence, 1920* | Edith Wharton (1862–1937)

The van der Luydens had done their best to emphasise the importance of the occasion. The du Lac Sevres and the Trevenna George II plate were out; so was the van der Luyden 'Lowestoft' (East India Company) and the Dagonet Crown Derby. Mrs. van der Luyden looked more than ever like a Cabanel, and Mrs. Archer, in her grandmother's seed-pearls and emeralds, reminded her son of an Isabey miniature. All the ladies had on their handsomest jewels, but it was characteristic of the house and the occasion that these were mostly in rather heavy old-fashioned settings; and old Miss Lanning, who had been persuaded to come, actually wore her mother's cameos and a Spanish blonde shawl.

The Countess Olenska was the only young woman at the dinner; yet, as Archer scanned the smooth plump elderly faces between their diamond necklaces and towering ostrich feathers, they struck him as curiously immature compared with hers. It frightened him to think what must have gone to the making of her eyes.

The Duke of St. Austrey, who sat at his hostess's right, was naturally the chief figure of the evening. But if the Countess Olenska was less conspicuous than had been hoped, the Duke was almost invisible. Being a well-bred man he had not (like another recent ducal visitor) come to the dinner in a shooting-jacket; but his evening clothes were so shabby and baggy, and he wore them with such an air of their being homespun, that (with his stooping way of sitting, and the vast beard spreading over his shirt-front) he hardly gave the appearance of being in dinner attire. He was short, round-shouldered, sunburnt, with a thick nose, small eyes and a sociable smile; but he seldom spoke, and when he did it was in such low tones that, despite the frequent silences of expectation about the table, his remarks were lost to all but his neighbours.

Dinner

From *Some Experiences of an Irish R.M., 1899* | Somerville & Ross

(Edith Somerville, 1858–1949, and Martin Ross / Violet Florence Martin, 1862–1915)

Dinner was as incongruous as everything else. Detestable soup in a splendid old silver tureen that was nearly as dark in hue as Robinson Crusoe's thumb; a perfect salmon, perfectly cooked, on a chipped kitchen dish; such cut glass as is not easy to find nowadays; sherry that, as Flurry subsequently remarked, would burn the shell off an egg; and a bottle of port, draped in immemorial cobwebs, wan with age, and probably priceless.

Rations

From *South: The Endurance Expedition, 1919*

Ernest Shackleton (1874–1922)

A little Cerebos salt had been saved, and this was issued out at the rate of three-quarters of an ounce per man per week. Some of the packets containing the salt had broken, so that all did not get the full ration. On the other hand, one man dropped his week's ration on the floor of the hut, amongst the stones and dirt. It was quickly collected, and he found to his delight that he had enough now to last him for three weeks. Of course it was not *all* salt. The hot drink consisted at first of milk made from milk-powder up to about one-quarter of its proper strength. This was later on diluted still more, and sometimes replaced by a drink made from a pea-soup-like packing from the Bovril sledging rations. For midwinter's day celebrations, a mixture of one teaspoonful of methylated spirit in a pint of hot water, flavoured with a little ginger and sugar, served to remind some of cock-tails and *Veuve Cliquot*.

Oberon's Feast

Robert Herrick (1591–1674)

Shapcot! to thee the Fairy State
I with discretion, dedicate.
Because thou prizest things that are
Curious and un-familiar.
Take first the feast; these dishes gone,
Wee'l see the Fairy-Court *anon.*

A little mushroome table spred,
After short prayers, they set on bread;
A Moon-parcht grain of purest wheat,
With some small glit'ring gritt, to eate
His choyce bitts with; then in a trice
They make a feast lesse great then nice.
But all this while his eye is serv'd,
We must not think his ear was sterv'd;
But that there was in place to stir
His Spleen, the chirring Grasshopper,
The merry Cricket, puling Flie,
The piping Gnat for minstralcy.
And now, we must imagine, first,
The Elves present, to quench his thirst,
A pure seed-Pearl of Infant dew
Brought and besweetened in a blew
And pregnant violet; which done,
His kitling eyes begin to runne
Quite through the table, where he spies
The hornes of paperie Butterflies,
Of which he eates, and tastes a little

Of that we call the Cuckoes spittle.
A little Fuz-ball pudding stands
By, yet not blessed by his hands,
That was too coorse; but then forthwith
He ventures boldly on the pith
Of sugred Rush, and eats the sagge
And well bestrutted Bees sweet bagge:
Gladdening his pallat with some store
Of Emits eggs; what wo'd he more?
But Beards of Mice, a Newts stew'd thigh,
A bloated Earewig, and a Flie;
With the Red-capt worme, that's shut
Within the concave of a Nut,
Brown as his Tooth. A little Moth
Late fattned in a piece of cloth:
With withered cherries; Mandrakes eares;
Moles eyes; to these the slain-Stags teares:
The unctuous dewlaps of a Snaile;
The broke-heart of a Nightingale
Ore-come in musicke; with a wine
Ne're ravisht from the flattering Vine,
But gently prest from the soft side
Of the most sweet and dainty Bride,
Brought in a dainty daizie, which
He fully quaffs up to bewitch
His blood to height; this done, commended
Grace by his Priest; *The feast is ended.*

NOVEMBER

Please Sir, I Want Some More

Good Toast

From *Kitchen Essays, 1922* | Agnes Jekyll (1861–1937)

Toast, to be good, demands a glowing grate, a handy toasting-fork, and a patient watcher – counsels of perfection indeed, for the ideal rack is like friendship and the immortality of the soul, almost too good to be true. An anxious bride, humiliated by the sort of toast only a starving sparrow could relish, wrote to one learned in such matters, asking for a trustworthy recipe.

'Cut a slice of bread, hold it before the fire and say incantations,' was the unhelpful but only advice vouchsafed. An electric griller can be used successfully by those who can successfully use such contraptions, but the elemental toasting-fork, the patient watcher before the fire, and a go-between, with the honour of the house at heart, are really the truest solution.

Toast

From *Toast, 2003* | Nigel Slater (1956–)

My mother is scraping a piece of burned toast out of the kitchen window, a crease of annoyance across her forehead. This is not an occasional occurrence, a once-in-a-while hiccup in a busy mother's day. My mother burns the toast as surely as the sun rises each morning. In fact, I doubt if she has ever made a round of toast in her life that has failed to fill the kitchen with plumes of throat-catching smoke. I am nine now and I have never seen butter without black bits in it.

It is impossible not to love someone who makes toast for you. People's failings, even major ones such as when they make you wear short trousers to school, fall into insignificance as your teeth break through the rough, toasted crust and sink into the doughy cushion of white bread underneath. Once the warm, salty butter hits your tongue, you are smitten. Putty in their hands.

We May Live Without Poetry

From *Lucile, Part I, Canto II* |

Edward Robert Bulwer Lytton / Owen Meredith (1831–1891)

XIX

We may live without poetry, music, and art;
We may live without conscience, and live without heart;
We may live without friends; we may live without books;
But civilised man cannot live without cooks.
He may live without books, – what is knowledge but grieving?
He may live without hope, – what is hope but deceiving?
He may live without love, – what is passion but pining?
But where is the man who can live without dining?

One Cannot Think Well

From *A Room of One's Own, 1929* | Virginia Woolf (1882–1941)

The human frame being what it is, heart, body and brain all mixed together, and not contained in separate compartments as they will be no doubt in another million years, a good dinner is of great importance to good talk. One cannot think well, love well, sleep well, if one has not dined well. The lamp in the spine does not light on beef and prunes.

Please, Sir

From *Oliver Twist, 1837* | Charles Dickens (1812–1870)

The evening arrived; the boys took their places. The master, in his cook's uniform, stationed himself at the copper; his pauper assistants ranged themselves behind him; the gruel was served out; and a long grace was said over the short commons. The gruel disappeared; the boys whispered to each other, and winked at Oliver; while his next neighbours nudged him. Child as he was, he was desperate with hunger, and reckless with misery. He rose from the table; and advancing to the master, basin and spoon in hand, said, somewhat alarmed at his own daring:

'Please, sir, I want some more.'

The master was a fat, healthy man; but he turned very pale. He gazed in stupefied astonishment on the small rebel for some seconds, and then clung for support to the copper. The assistants were paralysed with wonder; the boys with fear.

'What!' said the master at length, in a faint voice.

'Please, sir, I want some more.'

The master aimed a blow at Oliver's head with the ladle; pinioned him in his arm; and shrieked aloud for the beadle.

The board were sitting in solemn conclave, when Mr. Bumble rushed into the room in great excitement, and addressing the gentleman in the high chair, said:

'Mr. Limbkins, I beg your pardon, sir! Oliver Twist has asked for more!' There was a general start of horror.

'For *more*!' said Mr. Limbkins. 'Compose yourself, Bumble, and answer me distinctly. Do I understand that he asked for more, after he had eaten the supper allotted by the dietary?'

'He did, sir,' replied Bumble.

'That boy will be hung,' said the gentleman in the white waistcoat. 'I know that boy will be hung.'

Oysters

From *A Complete Collection of Genteel and Ingenious Conversation, Dialogue Two, 1738* | Jonathan Swift (1667–1745)

Lady Smart: Ladies and Gentlemen, will you eat any oysters before dinner?

Colonel Atwit: With all my Heart. [*Takes an oyster.*] He was a bold man, that first ate an oyster.

Lady Smart: They say oysters are a cruel meat, because we eat them alive: then they are an uncharitable meat, for we leave nothing to the poor; and they are an ungodly meat, because we never say grace.

Mr Neverout: Faith, that's as well said, as if I had said it myself.

Eating Oysters

From *The Walrus and the Carpenter, Through the Looking-Glass, 1871* | Lewis Carroll (1832–1898)

'O Oysters, come and walk with us!'
　　The Walrus did beseech.
'A pleasant walk, a pleasant talk,
　　Along the briny beach:
We cannot do with more than four,
　　To give a hand to each.'

The eldest Oyster looked at him.
　　But never a word he said:
The eldest Oyster winked his eye,
　　And shook his heavy head –
Meaning to say he did not choose
　　To leave the oyster-bed.

But four young oysters hurried up,
　　All eager for the treat:
Their coats were brushed, their faces washed,
　　Their shoes were clean and neat –
And this was odd, because, you know,
　　They hadn't any feet.

Four other Oysters followed them,
　　And yet another four;
And thick and fast they came at last,
　　And more, and more, and more –
All hopping through the frothy waves,
　　And scrambling to the shore.

The Walrus and the Carpenter
　　Walked on a mile or so,

And then they rested on a rock
    Conveniently low:
And all the little Oysters stood
    And waited in a row.

'The time has come,' the Walrus said,
    'To talk of many things:
Of shoes – and ships – and sealing-wax –
    Of cabbages – and kings –
And why the sea is boiling hot –
    And whether pigs have wings.'

'But wait a bit,' the Oysters cried,
    'Before we have our chat;
For some of us are out of breath,
    And all of us are fat!'
'No hurry!' said the Carpenter.
    They thanked him much for that.

'A loaf of bread,' the Walrus said,
    'Is what we chiefly need:
Pepper and vinegar besides
    Are very good indeed –
Now if you're ready Oysters dear,
    We can begin to feed.'

'But not on us!' the Oysters cried,
    Turning a little blue,
'After such kindness, that would be
    A dismal thing to do!'

'The night is fine,' the Walrus said
    'Do you admire the view?

'It was so kind of you to come!
    And you are very nice!'
The Carpenter said nothing but
    'Cut us another slice:
I wish you were not quite so deaf –
    I've had to ask you twice!'

'It seems a shame,' the Walrus said,
    'To play them such a trick,
After we've brought them out so far,
    And made them trot so quick!'
The Carpenter said nothing but
    'The butter's spread too thick!'

'I weep for you,' the Walrus said.
    'I deeply sympathize.'
With sobs and tears he sorted out
    Those of the largest size.
Holding his pocket handkerchief
    Before his streaming eyes.

'O Oysters,' said the Carpenter.
    'You've had a pleasant run!
Shall we be trotting home again?'
    But answer came there none –
And that was scarcely odd, because
    They'd eaten every one.'

Sucking Oranges

From *Cranford, 1853* | Elizabeth Gaskell (1810–1865)

When oranges came in, a curious proceeding was gone through.
Miss Jenkyns did not like to cut the fruit; for, as she observed,
the juice all ran out nobody knew where; sucking (only I think
she used some more recondite word) was in fact the only way of
enjoying oranges; but then there was the unpleasant association with
a ceremony frequently gone through by little babies; and so, after
dessert, in orange season, Miss Jenkyns and Miss Matty used to rise
up, possess themselves each of an orange in silence, and withdraw to
the privacy of their own rooms to indulge in sucking oranges.

I had once or twice tried, on such occasions, to prevail on Miss
Matty to stay, and had succeeded in her sister's lifetime. I held up
a screen, and did not look, and, as she said, she tried not to make the
noise very offensive; but now that she was left alone, she seemed quite
horrified when I begged her to remain with me in the warm dining-
parlour, and enjoy her orange as she liked best.

8 November

The Orange

Wendy Cope (1945–)

At lunchtime I bought a huge orange –
The size of it made us all laugh.
I peeled it and shared it with Robert and Dave –
They got quarters and I had a half.

And that orange, it made me so happy,
As ordinary things often do
Just lately. The shopping. A walk in the park.
This is peace and contentment. It's new.

The rest of the day was quite easy.
I did all the jobs on my list
And enjoyed them and had some time over.
I love you. I'm glad I exist.

Meat for Tea!

From *Riceyman Steps, 1923* | Arnold Bennett (1867–1931)

Violet displayed the contents of the under-plate, and showed that noses had not been wrong in assuming them to be a beef-steak; the steak was stewed; it was very attractive, seductive, full of sound nourishment; one would have deemed it irresistible. Violet rose and deposited the plate in front of Henry, who said nothing. She then bent over him, and with his knife and fork cut off a little corner from the meat.

'You're going to give this bit to your little wife,' she whispered endearingly, and kissed him, and sat down again with the bit, which she at once began to eat. 'It's very tender,' said she, pretending that the steak was a quite commonplace matter, that it was not unique, breathtaking, in the annals of tea-time in Riceyman Steps.

'I don't think I can eat any,' said Henry amiably.

'To please me,' Violet cajoled again, as at breakfast, changing her voice with all the considerable sexual charm at her disposition.

'I'm really not hungry,' said Henry.

'I shan't finish mine till you begin yours.' Her voice was now changing.

She waited for him to begin. He did not begin. The point with Henry was, not that he disliked the steak, but that for reasons of domestic policy he was absolutely determined not to eat it. Meat for tea! What an insane notion! The woman was getting ideas into her head! He saw in the steak the thin edge of a wedge. He felt that the time was crucial. He had been married for little less than a year, and he knew women. Placidly he continued with his bread-and-margarine.

Lemonade?

From *Anecdotes of Destiny: Babette's Feast, 1958*

Isak Dinesen / Karen Blixen (1885–1962)

At the dinner for the Dean's hundredth anniversary:
The boy once more filled the glasses. This time the Brothers and
Sisters knew that what they were given to drink was not wine, for it
sparkled. It must be some kind of lemonade. The lemonade agreed
with their exalted state of mind and seemed to lift them off the
ground, into a higher and purer sphere.

General Loewenhielm again set down his glass, turned to his
neighbor on the right and said to him: 'But surely this is a Veuve
Cliquot 1860?' His neighbor looked at him kindly, smiled at him
and made a remark about the weather.

Can You Cook Creole?

From *Gather Together in My Name, 1974* | Maya Angelou (1928–2014)

'Can you cook Creole?'

I looked at the woman and gave her a lie as soft as melting butter. 'Yes, of course. That's all I know how to cook.'

The Creole Café had a cardboard sign in the window which bragged: COOK WANTED. SEVENTY-FIVE DOLLARS A WEEK. As soon as I saw it I knew I could cook Creole, whatever that was.

. . . .

I asked Old Papa Ford to teach me how to cook:

'Why the sheeit do you want to work in a goddam kitchen?'

'Papa, the job pays seventy-five dollars a week.'

'Busting some goddam sude.' Disgust wrinkled his face.

'Papa, I'll be cooking and not washing dishes.'

'Colored women been cooking so long, thought you'd be tired of it by now.'

'If you'll just tell me – '

'Got all that education. How come you don't get a goddam job where you can go to work looking like something?'

I tried another tack. 'I probably couldn't learn to cook Creole food, anyway. It's too complicated.'

'Sheeit. Ain't nothing but onions, green peppers and garlic. Put that in everything and you've got Creole food. You know how to cook rice, don't you?'

'Yes,' I could cook it till each grain stood separately.

'That's all then. Them geechees can't live without swamp seed.' He cackled at his joke, then recalled a frown. 'Still don't like you working as a goddam cook. Get married, then you don't have to cook for nobody but your own family.'

Onions

Jonathan Swift (1667–1745)

Come, follow me by the smell,
  Here are delicate onions to sell;
I promise to use you well.
  They make the blood warmer,
  You'll feed like a farmer;
For this is every cook's opinion,
No savoury dish without an onion;
But, lest your kissing should be spoil'd,
Your onions must be thoroughly boil'd:
  Or else you may spare
  Your mistress a share,
The secret will never be known:
  She cannot discover
  The breath of her lover,
But think it as sweet as her own.

Trishna, Bombay's Favourite Seafood Spot

From *Dishoom*, 2019

Shamil Thakrar (1971–), Kavi Thakrar (1982–) and Naved Nasir (1979–)

The interior is dimly lit, but nonetheless welcoming. You will be seated in one of two rooms, one pleasant and rather unremarkable, the other happily deliberate in its marine-themed design. The dishes you are about to eat should (hopefully) owe their existence to the sea, and the room will no doubt remind you of this in case you forget.

Questions of décor aside, turn your attention to where it should be – on the food. Though the koliwada (pieces of fish or seafood cooked in a spicy batter) is excellent, and should be sampled, the main event is the famous 'butter pepper garlic crab'. If you lust after all these ingredients individually, you will appreciate the helpful transparency of the dish's name. Having chosen your spiny beast from the selection offered by the enthusiastic waiters, you wave it goodbye and await its demise and subsequent preparation. It will return so thoroughly immersed in butter, pepper and garlic that you wouldn't raise an eyebrow if it started speaking French. Take up your cracker, pick up your pick, and set to work. Don't be afraid to crunch away with gusto. Everyone else will be doing the same. You mustn't be put off, however, if you are not a fan of dismantling whole crustaceans. It is certainly possible, if less satisfying, to ask for the crab neatly pre-shelled. Make your choice according to your levels of energy, enthusiasm or squeamishness.

Necessaries and Luxuries of Life

From *Walden, 1854* | Henry David Thoreau (1817–1862)

One farmer says to me, 'You cannot live on vegetable food solely, for it furnishes nothing to make bones with;' and so he religiously devotes a part of his day to supplying his system with the raw material of bones; walking all the while he talks behind his oxen, which, with vegetable-made bones, jerk him and his lumbering plough along in spite of every obstacle. Some things are really necessaries of life in some circles, the most helpless and diseased, which in others are luxuries merely, and in others still are entirely unknown.

The Pleasure of Hunger

From *The Compleat Angler, Part I, 1653–1676*

Izaak Walton (1593–1683)

Venator: Poor men, and those that fast often, have much more pleasure in eating than rich men, and gluttons, that always feed before their stomachs are empty of their last meat and call for more; for by that means they rob themselves of that pleasure that hunger brings to poor men.

How Pleasant it is to Have Money

From *Dipsychus* | Arthur Hugh Clough (1819–1861)

Spirit:
As I sat at the café, I said to myself,
They may talk as they please about what they call pelf,
They may sneer as they like about eating and drinking,
But help it I cannot, I cannot help thinking
    How pleasant it is to have money, heigh ho!
    How pleasant it is to have money.

I sit at my table *en grand seigneur*,
And when I have done, throw a crust to the poor;
Not only the pleasure, one's self, of good living,
But also the pleasure of now and then giving.
    So pleasant it is to have money, heigh ho!
    So pleasant it is to have money.

Cooking Beneath the Ocean

From *The Sea Fairies, 1911* | L. Frank Baum (1856–1919)

'Our dinner is at noon, for we have to cook in the middle of the day, when the sun is shining,' she [the mermaid] said.

'Cook!' cried Trot; 'why, you can't build a fire in the water, can you?'

'We have no need of fires,' was the reply. 'The glass roof of our kitchen is so curved that it concentrates the heat of the sun's rays, which are then hot enough to cook anything we wish.'

'But how do you get along if the day is cloudy, and the sun doesn't shine?' inquired the little girl.

'Then we use the hot springs that bubble up in another part of the palace,' Merla answered. 'But the sun is the best to cook by.'

The Season of Happiness

From *Confessions of an English Opium Eater, 1821*

Thomas De Quincey (1785–1859)

From the latter weeks of October to Christmas-eve, therefore, is the
period during which happiness is in season, which, in my judgment,
enters the room with the tea-tray: for tea, though ridiculed by those
who are naturally of coarse nerves, or are become so from wine-
drinking, and are not susceptible of influence from so refined a
stimulant, will always be the favourite beverage of the intellectual.

An Indian Dish

From *Vanity Fair*, 1847–8 | William Makepeace Thackeray (1811–1863)

Mrs. Sedley had prepared a fine curry for her son, just as he liked it, and in the course of dinner a portion of this dish was offered to Rebecca. 'What is it?' said she, turning an appealing look to Mr. Joseph.

'Capital,' said he. His mouth was full of it: his face quite red with the delightful exercise of gobbling. 'Mother, it's as good as my own curries in India.'

'Oh, I must try some, if it is an Indian dish,' said Miss Rebecca. 'I am sure everything must be good that comes from there.'

'Give Miss Sharp some curry, my dear,' said Mr. Sedley, laughing. Rebecca had never tasted the dish before.

'Do you find it as good as everything else from India?' said Mr. Sedley.

'Oh, excellent!' said Rebecca, who was suffering tortures with the cayenne pepper.

'Try a chili with it, Miss Sharp,' said Joseph, really interested.

'A chili,' said Rebecca, gasping. 'Oh yes!' She thought a chili was something cool, as its name imported, and was served with some. 'How fresh and green they look,' she said, and put one into her mouth. It was hotter than the curry; flesh and blood could bear it no longer. She laid down her fork. 'Water, for Heaven's sake, water!' she cried. Mr. Sedley burst out laughing (he was a coarse man, from the Stock Exchange, where they love all sorts of practical jokes). 'They are real Indian, I assure you,' said he. 'Give Miss Sharp some water.'

Introduction

From *The Anatomy of Dessert, 1929*

Edward Bunyard (1878–1939)

In the vast literature which deals with food and its appreciation
I have searched for thirty years to find a precedent for a book devoted
to the dessert.

The great classic authors of France have left it untouched, nor can
I find in any language a treatise on this crucial subject, which may so
easily make or mar a well-planned meal.

How often after a dinner ordered with intelligence, prepared with
art and served with discretion, do we dwindle to a dessert unworthy
of its setting. Who has not encountered the Jonathan Apple or
the Jamaican Banana at a table which would scorn to provide an
unacknowledged St. Julien or an invalid Port?

It seems, therefore, there may be a need for a book of the dessert
such as this, but I write it under disadvantages which no gustronomic
scribe has faced since the time of Moses.

I have no one to copy.

(Gustronomy, usually spelled Gastronomy – from the Greek *gaster*, a
belly. As the Epicure's life is devoted this crude organ its place, and
placing taste first, I suggest that gustronomy is a better word, more
correct, decent, and desirable.)

The Publisher's Pudding

From *Modern Cookery for Private Families, 1845*

Eliza Acton (1799–1859)

This pudding can scarcely be made *too rich*. First blanch, and then
beat to the smoothest possible paste, six ounces of fresh Jordan
almonds, and a dozen bitter ones; pour very gradually to them, in
the mortar, three quarters of a pint of boiling cream; then turn them
into a cloth, and wring it from them again with strong expression.
Heat a full half pint of it afresh, and pour it, as soon as it boils, upon
four ounces of fine bread-crumbs, set a plate over, and leave them
to become nearly cold; then mix thoroughly with them four ounces
of macaroons, crushed tolerably small; five of finely minced beef-
suet, five of marrow, cleared very carefully from fibre, and from the
splinters of bone which are sometimes found in it, and shred not
very small, two ounces of flour, six of pounded sugar, four of dried
cherries, four of the best Muscatel raisins, weighed after they are
stoned, half a pound of candied citron, or of citron and orange-rind
mixed, a quarter saltspoonful of salt, half a nutmeg, the yolks only of
seven full-sized eggs, the grated rind of a large lemon, and last of all,
a glass of the best Cognac brandy, which must be stirred briskly in by
slow decrees. Pour the mixture into a *thickly* buttered mould or basin,
which contains a full quart, fill it to the brim, lay a sheet of buttered
writing-paper over, then a well-floured cloth, tie them securely, and
boil the pudding for four hours and a quarter; let it stand for two
minutes before it is turned out; dish it carefully.

The Poor Author's Pudding

From *Modern Cookery for Private Families*, 1845

Eliza Acton (1799–1859)

Flavour a quart of new milk by boiling in it for a few minutes half
a stick of well-bruised cinnamon, or the thin rind of a small lemon;
add a few grains of salt, and three ounces of sugar, and turn the
whole into a deep basin; when it is quite cold, stir to it three well-
beaten eggs, and strain the mixture into a pie-dish. Cover the top
entirely with slices of bread free from crust, and half an inch thick,
cut so as to join neatly, and buttered on both sides: bake the
pudding in a moderate oven for about half an hour, or in a Dutch
oven before the fire.

23 November

Thanksgiving

From A Lady's Life in the Rocky Mountains, 1879

Isabella Bird (1831–1904)

We spent the afternoon cooking the Thanksgiving dinner. I made
a wonderful pudding, for which I had saved eggs and cream for
days, and dried and stoned cherries supplied the place of currants.
I made a bowl of custard for sauce, which the men said was
'splendid'; also a rolled pudding, with molasses; and we had venison
steak and potatoes, but for tea we were obliged to use the tea leaves of
the morning again. I should think that few people in America have
enjoyed their Thanksgiving dinner more.

24 November

The Olive Crop

From *Perfume from Provence, 1935* | Winifred Fortescue (1888–1951)

To the great disappointment of Monsieur, our olives did not fill
sixteen measures, and therefore our crop was not considered worthy
of being crushed separately. We were told that we could either sell
our olives at the mill, exchange them for the equivalent in oil, or mix
our crop with that of a neighbour to make up the required amount.
This we did, and, from the musty flavour of our share of the resulting
oil, our neighbour had evidently not worked 'with conscience,'
but had mixed mouldy and damaged fruit with the good olives.
However, we enjoyed the olive harvest and the visit to the old mill,
and we resolved to prune our neglected olive-trees to let the sunlight
into the centres and so get a better crop the following year.

Dried Mushrooms

From *My Ántonia, 1918* | Willa Cather (1873–1947)

That night, while grandmother was getting supper, we opened the package Mrs. Shimerda had given her. It was full of little brown chips that looked like the shavings of some root. They were as light as feathers, and the most noticeable thing about them was their penetrating, earthy odour. We could not determine whether they were animal or vegetable.

'They might be dried meat from some queer beast, Jim. They ain't dried fish, and they never grew on stalk or vine. I'm afraid of 'em. Anyhow, I shouldn't want to eat anything that had been shut up for months with old clothes and goose pillows.'

She threw the package into the stove, but I bit off a corner of one of the chips I held in my hand, and chewed it tentatively. I never forgot the strange taste; though it was many years before I knew that those little brown shavings, which the Shimerdas had brought so far and treasured so jealously, were dried mushrooms. They had been gathered, probably, in some deep Bohemian forest …

The Mock Turtle

From *Alice's Adventures in Wonderland, 1865*

Lewis Carroll (1832–1898)

The Mock Turtle sighed deeply, and began, in a voice
sometimes choked with sobs, to sing this:–

'Beautiful Soup, so rich and green,
Waiting in a hot tureen!
Who for such dainties would not stoop?
Soup of the evening, beautiful Soup!
Soup of the evening, beautiful Soup!
    Beau – ootiful Soo – oop!
    Beau – ootiful Soo – oop!
Soo – oop of the e – e – evening,
    Beautiful, beautiful Soup!

'Beautiful Soup! Who cares for fish,
Game, or any other dish?
Who would not give all else for two
    pennyworth only of beautiful Soup?
Pennyworth only of beautiful Soup?
    Beau – ootiful Soo – oop!
    Beau – ootiful Soo – oop!
Soo – oop of the e – e – evening,
    Beautiful, beauti – FUL SOUP!'

Inspiration from Alice

From *Historic Heston, 2013* | Heston Blumenthal (1966–)

I went back to *Alice* for inspiration, leafing past the White Rabbit
– 'oh my ears and whiskers, how late it's getting' – and the hookah-
smoking caterpillar; past the Duchess and the Cheshire Cat; past the
Mad Hatter and the March Hare taking tea, until I reached chapter
9. And there it was, staring at me from Tenniel's classic illustration of
the Mock Turtle.

I'd read the book many times. I'd seen the drawing many times.
But it was only now that it dawned on me exactly what I was looking
at, and it was a revelation. The head that stuck out of the turtle's shell
was a calf's head. The back flippers were in fact hooves, and a calf's
tail dangled behind it. It wasn't a turtle but a mock turtle. Tenniel's
fantasy creature cleverly alluded to the ingredients of the soup, so
why couldn't I reverse the process and create a soup that alluded to
features of Carroll's story?

28 November

Cayenne Gingerbread

From *A Lady's Life in the Rocky Mountains, 1879*

Isabella Bird (1831–1904)

November 29

Before the boy came I had mistaken some faded cayenne pepper
for ginger, and had made a cake with it. Last evening I put half of
it into the cupboard and left the door open. During the night we
heard a commotion in the kitchen and much choking, coughing, and
groaning, and at breakfast the boy was unable to swallow food with
his usual ravenousness. After breakfast he came to me whimpering,
and asking for something soothing for his throat, admitting that he
had seen the 'gingerbread,' and 'felt so starved' in the night that he
got up to eat it.

I tried to make him feel that it was 'real mean' to eat so much and
be so useless, and he said he would do anything to help me, but the
men were so 'down on him.' I never saw men so patient with a lad
before. He is a most vexing addition to our party, yet one cannot help
laughing at him.

A Scotch Breakfast

From *Waverley, 1814* | Sir Walter Scott (1771–1832)

He [Waverley] found Miss Bradwardine presiding over the tea and
coffee, the table loaded with warm bread, both of flour, oatmeal,
and barley-meal, in the shape of loaves, cakes, biscuits, and other
varieties, together with eggs, rein-deer ham, mutton and beef ditto,
smoked salmon, marmalade, and all the other delicacies which
induced even Johnson himself to extol the luxury of a Scotch
breakfast above that of all other countries. A mess of oatmeal
porridge, flanked by a silver jug, which held an equal mixture of
cream and butter-milk, was placed for the Baron's share of this repast.

DECEMBER

The Delights of the Season

Vintners

From *The Rubáiyát of Omar Khayyám, 1859*

Omar ibn Ibrahim al-Khayyám (1048–1131)

Translated by Edward FitzGerald (1809–1883)

LXXI

And much as Wine has play'd the Infidel,
And robb'd me of my Robe of Honour – well,
   I often wonder what the Vintners buy
One half so precious as the Goods they sell.

Inviting a Friend to Supper

Ben Jonson (1572–1637)

To night, grave sir, both my poore house, and I
Doe equally desire your companie:
Not that we thinke us worthy such a ghest,
But that your worth will dignifie our feast,
With those that come; whose grace may make that seeme
Something, which else, could hope for no esteeme.
It is the faire acceptance, Sir, creates
The entertaynment perfect: not the cates.
Yet shall you have, to rectifie your palate,
An olive, capers, or some better sallade
Ushring the mutton; with a short-leg'd hen,
If we can get her, full of egs, and then
Limons, and wine for sauce: to these a coney
Is not to be despair'd of, for our money;
And, though fowle, now, be scarce, yet there are clarkes,
The skie not falling, thinke we may have larkes.
Ile tell you more, and lye, so you will come:
Of partrich, pheasant, wood-cock, of which some
May yet be there; and godwit, if we can:
Knat, raile, and ruffe too. How so ere, my man
Shall reade a piece of Virgil, Tacitus,
Livie, or of some better booke to us,

Of which wee'll speak our minds, amidst our meate;
And Ile professe no verses to repeate:
To this, if ought appeare which I not know of,
That will the pastrie, not my paper, show of.
Digestive cheese and fruit there sure will bee;
But that, which most doth take my Muse and mee,
Is a pure cup of rich Canary-wine,
Which is the Mermaids now, but shall be mine:
Of which had Horace, or Anacreon tasted,
Their lives, as doe their lines, till now had lasted.
Tobacco, Nectar, or the Thespian spring,
Are all but Luthers beere to this I sing.
Of this we will sup free, but moderately,
And we will have no Pooly', or Parrot by;
Nor shall our cups make any guiltie men;
But, at our parting we will be, as when
We innocently met. No simple word,
That shall be utter'd at our mirthfull boord,
Shall make us sad next morning: or affright
The libertie that wee'll enjoy to night.

Dinner at Mole End

From *The Wind in the Willows, 1908* | Kenneth Grahame (1859–1932)

'Rat,' he [Mole] moaned, 'how about your supper, you poor, cold, hungry, weary animal? I've nothing to give you – nothing – not a crumb!'

'What a fellow you are for giving in!' said the Rat reproachfully. 'Why, only just now I saw a sardine-opener on the kitchen dresser, quite distinctly; and everybody knows that means there are sardines about somewhere in the neighbourhood. Rouse yourself! pull yourself together, and come with me and forage.'

They went and foraged accordingly, hunting through every cupboard and turning out every drawer. The result was not so very depressing after all, though of course it might have been better; a tin of sardines – a box of captain's biscuits, nearly full – and a German sausage encased in silver paper.

'There's a banquet for you!' observed the Rat, as he arranged the table. 'I know some animals who would give their ears to be sitting down to supper with us to-night!'

'No bread!' groaned the Mole dolorously; 'no butter, no –'

'No *pâté de foie gras*, no champagne!' continued the Rat, grinning. 'And that reminds me – what's that little door at the end of the passage? Your cellar, of course! Every luxury in this house! Just you wait a minute.'

He made for the cellar-door, and presently reappeared, somewhat dusty, with a bottle of beer in each paw and another under each arm, 'Self-indulgent beggar you seem to be, Mole,' he observed. 'Deny yourself nothing. This is really the jolliest little place I ever was in.'

How to Eat Muffins

From *The Importance of Being Earnest, 1895*

Oscar Wilde (1854–1900)

ALGERNON:

I can't eat muffins in an agitated manner. The butter would probably get on my cuffs. One should always eat muffins quite calmly. It is the only way to eat them.

An English Muffin

From *Paris and the Parisians, 1836* | Fanny Trollope (1779–1863)

A Frenchman's response on being offered an English bun:
'No, no! it is enough to look at them!' said her cavalier, almost
shuddering. 'There is no lightness, no elegance, no grace in any single
gâteau here.'

'Mais goûtez quelque chose,' reiterated the lady.

'Vous le voulez absolument!' exclaimed the young man; 'quelle
tyrannic! … and what a proof of obedience I am about to give
you! … Voyons donc!' he continued, approaching a plate on which
were piled some truly English muffins which, as you know, are
of a somewhat mysterious manufacture, and about as palatable
if eaten untoasted as a slice from a leathern glove. To this *gâteau*,
as he supposed it to be, the unfortunate connoisseur in patisserie
approached, exclaiming with rather a theatrical air, 'Voilà donc ce
que je vais faire pour vos beaux yeux!'

As he spoke, he took up one of the pale, tough things, and, to our
extreme amusement, attempted to eat it. Any one might be excused
for making a few grimaces on such an occasion, and a Frenchman's
privilege in this line is well known: but this hardy experimentalist
outdid this privilege;– he was in a perfect agony, and his spittings and
reproachings were so vehement that friends, strangers, boutiquier,
and all, even down to a little befloured urchin who entered at the
moment with a tray of patties, burst into uncontrollable laughter,
which the unfortunate, to do him justice, bore with extreme good
humour, only making his fair countrywoman promise that she would
never insist upon his eating English confectionary again.

Making the Most of the Whole Beast

From *Nose to Tail Eating, 1999* | Fergus Henderson (1963–)

'Nose to Tail Eating' means it would be disingenuous to the animal not to make the most of the whole beast; there is a set of delights, textural and flavoursome, which lie beyond the fillet.

This is a book about cooking and eating at home with friends and relations, not replicating restaurant plates of food.

Do not be afraid of cooking, as your ingredients will know, and misbehave. Enjoy your cooking and the food will behave; moreover it will pass your pleasure on to those who eat it.

6 December

Delights of the Seasons

From *Good Things, 1971* | Jane Grigson (1928–1990)

On frozen, canned and packaged food:
I think we should be thankful for being relieved of the famines
and inconvenience that the seasons used to bring to so many
communities. I have no patience with food Puritanism of that kind
(though I do wonder why the run of frozen food is not better – why
so many tasteless sliced beans, when one could have *haricot verts*?)

Having said this, and always being grateful for the background
of an unfailing larder, I feel that delight lies in the seasons and what
they bring us. One does not remember the grilled hamburgers and
frozen peas, but the strawberries that come in May and June straight
from the fields, the asparagus of a special occasion, kippers from
Craster in July and August, the first lamb of the year from Wales,
in October the fresh walnuts from France where they are eaten with
new cloudy wine. This is good food. The sad thing is that, unless we
fight, and demand, and complain, and reject, and generally make
ourselves thoroughly unpopular, these delights may be unknown
to our great-grandchildren. Perhaps even to our grandchildren. It is
certainly more convenient with growing populations, to freeze the
asparagus and strawberries straight from the ground, to dye and wrap
the kippers in plastic, to import hard, red, frozen lamb from New
Zealand and to push the walnuts straight into the drying kilns. It
is easier to put no seasoning to speak of into a sausage – it offends
nobody, everybody buys it. This is the theory. We're back to the
primitive idea of eating to stay alive.

7 December

Swedes

Edward Thomas (1878–1917)

They have taken the gable from the roof of clay
On the long swede pile. They have let in the sun
To the white and gold and purple of curled fronds
Unsunned. It is a sight more tender-gorgeous
At the wood-corner where Winter moans and drips
Than when, in the Valley of the Tombs of Kings,
A boy crawls down into a Pharaoh's tomb
And, first of Christian men, beholds the mummy,
God and monkey, chariot and throne and vase,
Blue pottery, alabaster, and gold.

But dreamless long-dead Amen-hotep lies.
This is a dream of Winter, sweet as Spring.

Roasting Apples and Chestnuts

From *London Labour and the London Poor, 1851*

Henry Mayhew (1812–1887)

Most of the fruit-stalls are, in the winter time, fitted up with an apparatus for roasting apples and chestnuts; this generally consists of an old saucepan with a fire inside; and the woman who vends them, huddled up in her old faded shawl or cloak, often presents a picturesque appearance, in the early evening, or in a fog, with the gleam of the fire lighting up her half somnolent figure. Within the last two or three years, however, there has been so large a business carried on in roasted chestnuts, that it has become a distinct street-trade, and the vendors have provided themselves with an iron apparatus, large enough to roast nearly half a bushel at a time. At the present time, however, the larger apparatus is less common in the streets, and more frequent in the shops, than in the previous winter.

9 December

Sugars

From *A New System of Domestic Cookery, 1806, 1816* |

A Lady / Mrs Rundell (1745–1828)

Sugars being an article of considerable expence in all families, the purchase demands particular attention. The cheapest does not go as far as that more refined; and there is difference even in the degree of sweetness. The white should be chosen that is close, heavy, and shining. The best sort of brown has a bright gravelly look, and is often to be bought pure as imported. East India sugars are finer for the price, but not so strong, consequently unfit for wines and sweetmeats but do well for common purposes, if good of their kind. To prepare white sugar, pounded, rolling it with a bottle, and sifting, wastes less than a mortar.

Haschich Fudge

From *The Alice B. Toklas Cook Book: Recipes with Friends,*
1954 | Alice B. Toklas (1877–1967), Brian Gysin (1916–1986)

(which anyone could whip up on a rainy day)

This is the food of Paradise – of Baudelaire's Artificial Paradises: it might provide an entertaining refreshment for a Ladies' Bridge Club or a chapter meeting of the DAR. In Morocco it is thought to be good for warding off the common cold in damp winter weather and is, indeed, more effective if taken with large quantities of hot mint tea. Euphoria and brilliant storms of laughter; ecstatic reveries and extension of one's personality on several simultaneous planes are to be complacently expected. Almost anything Saint Theresa did, you can do better if you can bear to be ravished by '*un évanouissement reveillé.*'

Take 1 teaspoon black peppercorns, 1 whole nutmeg, 4 average sticks of cinnamon, 1 teaspoon coriander. These should all be pulverised in a mortar. About a handful each of stoned dates, dried figs, shelled almonds and peanuts: chop these and mix them together. A bunch of *canibis sativ*a can be pulverised. This along with the spices should be dusted over the mixed fruit and nuts, kneaded together. About a cup of sugar dissolved in a big pat of butter. Rolled into a cake and cut into pieces or made into balls about the size of a walnut, it should be eaten with care. Two pieces are quite sufficient.

Obtaining the *canibis* may present certain difficulties, but the variety known as *canibis sativa* grows as a common weed, often unrecognized, everywhere in Europe, Asia and parts of Africa; besides being cultivated as a crop for the manufacture of rope. In the Americas, while often discouraged, its cousin, called *canibis indica*, has been observed even in city window boxes. It should be picked and dried as soon as it has gone to seed and while the plant is still green.

Breakfast

From *The Warden: Plumstead Episcopi, 1855*

Anthony Trollope (1815–1882)

And now let us observe the well-furnished breakfast-parlour at Plumstead Episcopi, and the comfortable air of all the belongings of the rectory. Comfortable they certainly were, but neither gorgeous nor even grand; indeed, considering the money that had been spent there, the eye and taste might have been better served; there was an air of heaviness about the rooms which might have been avoided without any sacrifice of propriety; colours might have been better chosen and lights more perfectly diffused; but perhaps in doing so the thorough clerical aspect of the whole might have been somewhat marred; at any rate, it was not without ample consideration that those thick, dark, costly carpets were put down; those embossed, but sombre papers hung up; those heavy curtains draped so as to half exclude the light of the sun: nor were these old-fashioned chairs, bought at a price far exceeding that now given for more modern goods, without a purpose. The breakfast-service on the table was equally costly and equally plain; the apparent object had been to spend money without obtaining brilliancy or splendour. The urn was of thick and solid silver, as were also the teapot, coffeepot, cream-ewer, and sugar-bowl; the cups were old, dim dragon china, worth about a pound a piece, but very despicable in the eyes of the uninitiated. The silver forks were so heavy as to be disagreeable to the hand, and the breadbasket was of a weight really formidable to any but robust persons. The tea consumed was the very best, the coffee the very blackest, the cream the very thickest; there was dry toast and buttered toast, muffins and crumpets; hot bread and cold bread, white bread and brown bread, home-made bread and bakers' bread, wheaten bread and oaten bread; and if there be other breads than these, they were there; there were eggs in napkins, and crispy bits of bacon under silver covers; and there were little fishes in a little box, and devilled kidneys frizzling on a hot-water dish; which, by the bye, were placed closely contiguous to the plate of the worthy archdeacon himself. Over and above this, on a snow-white napkin, spread upon the sideboard, was a huge ham and a huge sirloin; the latter having laden the dinner table on the previous evening. Such was the ordinary fare at Plumstead Episcopi.

Tea and Cake

From *Remembrance of Things Past: Du côté de chez Swann, 1913 (France), Swann's Way, 1922 (UK)* | Marcel Proust (1871–1922)

Translated by C. K. Scott Moncrieff (1889–1930)

Ouverture

Many years had elapsed during which nothing of Combray, save what was comprised in the theatre and the drama of my going to bed there, had any existence for me, when one day in winter, as I came home, my mother, seeing that I was cold, offered me some tea, a thing I did not ordinarily take. I declined at first, and then, for no particular reason, changed my mind. She sent out for one of those short, plump little cakes called 'petites madeleines,' which look as though they had been moulded in the fluted scallop of a pilgrim's shell. And soon, mechanically, weary after a dull day with the prospect of a depressing morrow, I raised to my lips a spoonful of the tea in which I had soaked a morsel of the cake. No sooner had the warm liquid, and the crumbs with it, touched my palate than a shudder ran through my whole body, and I stopped, intent upon the extraordinary changes that were taking place. An exquisite pleasure had invaded my senses, but individual, detached, with no suggestion of its origin. And at once the vicissitudes of life had become indifferent to me, its disasters innocuous, its brevity illusory – this new sensation having had on me the effect which love has of filling me with a precious essence; or rather this essence was not in me, it was myself. I had ceased now to feel mediocre, accidental, mortal. Whence could it have come to me, this all-powerful joy? I was conscious that it was connected with the taste of tea and cake, but that it infinitely transcended those savours, could not, indeed, be of the same nature as theirs. Whence did it come? What did it signify? How could I seize upon and define it?

An Unusual Dish

From *The Adventure of the Naval Treaty, 1893*

Sir Arthur Conan Doyle (1859–1930)

Mr Phelps and Watson wait for Holmes to solve the mystery of the Naval Treaty:

'After breakfast, my dear Watson. Remember that I have breathed thirty miles of Surrey air this morning. I suppose that there has been no answer from my cabman advertisement? Well, well, we cannot expect to score every time.'

The table was all laid, and just as I was about to ring Mrs. Hudson entered with the tea and coffee. A few minutes later she brought in three covers, and we all drew up to the table, Holmes ravenous, I curious, and Phelps in the gloomiest state of depression.

'Mrs. Hudson has risen to the occasion,' said Holmes, uncovering a dish of curried chicken. 'Her cuisine is a little limited, but she has as good an idea of breakfast as a Scotch-woman. What have you here, Watson?'

'Ham and eggs,' I answered.

'Good! What are you going to take, Mr. Phelps - curried fowl or eggs, or will you help yourself?'

'Thank you. I can eat nothing,' said Phelps.

'Oh, come! Try the dish before you.'

'Thank you, I would really rather not.'

'Well, then,' said Holmes, with a mischievous twinkle, 'I suppose that you have no objection to helping me?'

Phelps raised the cover, and as he did so he uttered a scream, and sat there staring with a face as white as the plate upon which he looked. Across the centre of it was lying a little cylinder of blue-grey paper. He caught it up, devoured it with his eyes, and then danced madly about the room, pressing it to his bosom and shrieking out in his delight. Then he fell back into an armchair so limp and exhausted with his own emotions that we had to pour brandy down his throat to keep him from fainting.

'There! there!' said Holmes, soothing, patting him upon the shoulder. 'It was too bad to spring it on you like this, but Watson here will tell you that I never can resist a touch of the dramatic.'

Phelps seized his hand and kissed it. 'God bless you!' he cried. 'You have saved my honour.'

'Well, my own was at stake, you know,' said Holmes. 'I assure you it is just as hateful to me to fail in a case as it can be to you to blunder over a commission.'

Phelps thrust away the precious document into the innermost pocket of his coat.

'I have not the heart to interrupt your breakfast any further, and yet I am dying to know how you got it and where it was.'

Sherlock Holmes swallowed a cup of coffee, and turned his attention to the ham and eggs. Then he rose, lit his pipe, and settled himself down into his chair.

Good Food

From *How to Eat, 1998* | Nigella Lawson (1960–)

Good food doesn't have to be difficult to cook, and it certainly doesn't need to be difficult to buy. But you must know what you're after. The important thing is to be greedy enough to get what's good, but not so restlessly greedy that you get too much of it. Restrict your choices so that you provide lots of a few things rather than small amounts of many. This is partly an aesthetic dictate, partly a practical one. If you buy 100g slices of six different cheeses, everyone is going to feel inhibited about cutting some off; however generous you have been, it is only the meagreness of each portion that will be apparent. Provide, instead, a semblance – indeed the reality – of voluptuous abundance. You don't need to buy more than three different cheeses, but get great big fat wodges of each. You want munificence, you want plenty, you want people to feel they can eat as much as they want and there'll still be some left over afterwards. Start by thinking along the lines of one hard cheese, one soft cheese and maybe a blue cheese or chèvre. You needn't stick to this rigidly: sometimes it's good just to be seduced by the particular cheeses spread out in front of you on a cheese counter. Keep your head, though: without ruling out whim entirely, don't be immoderately ensnared by fanciful names or the provocatively unfamiliar. One type of cheese no one has heard of might well be interesting, but not three. Anyway, the desire to be interesting is possibly the most damaging impulse in cooking. Never worry about what your guests will think of you. Just think of the food. Will it taste good?

Whales and Porpoises

From *Moby Dick, 1851* | Herman Melville (1819–1891)

It is upon record, that three centuries ago the tongue of the Right Whale was esteemed a great delicacy in France, and commanded large prices there. Also, that in Henry VIIIth's time, a certain cook of the court obtained a handsome reward for inventing an admirable sauce to be eaten with barbacued porpoises, which, you remember, are a species of whale. Porpoises, indeed, are to this day considered fine eating. The meat is made into balls about the size of billiard balls, and being well seasoned and spiced might be taken for turtle-balls or veal balls. The old monks of Dunfermline were very fond of them. They had a great porpoise grant from the crown.

The fact is, that among his hunters at least, the whale would by all hands be considered a noble dish, were there not so much of him; but when you come to sit down before a meat-pie nearly one hundred feet long, it takes away your appetite.

Athol Brose

Thomas Hood (1799–1845)

Charm'd with a drink which Highlanders compose,
    A German traveller exclaim'd with glee, –
'Potztausend! sare, if dis is Athol Brose,
    How goot dere Athol Boetry must be!'

Garlic

From *Freud on Food, 1978* | Clement Freud (1924–2009)

'Garlick hath properties,' wrote Thomas Nash in *The Unfortunate Traveller* (1594), 'that make a man winke, drinke and stinke.' In Nash's day, the 'stinke' was of no great importance; just another of a whole series of revolting smells two hundred years before the toothbrush, a hundred before soap, when a bath was considered eccentric, and a change of shirt made news. As personal hygiene became more generally accepted, garlic, by virtue of the 'stinke', became less and less common in this country, the aroma placing a man way down the social scale among poorman-beggarman-thief, to which must be added 'foreigner'. Now the acrid breath of garlic emanates from the best people as a status symbol of gastronomic emancipation. Enlightened young men, who in the thirties published slim leatherbound volumes of verse now run garlic and fishnet restaurants in SW3. Apart from what it does to your personal appeal, the best reason for NOT eating garlic is the fierceness of the residual patina, coating tongue and palate and tainting food and drink that follows. Of one thing there can be no doubt: meals that include dishes cooked with garlic must be most carefully considered. A dish of hot garlic bread followed by melon; an aioli of prawns before a hot house peach is not only hard on the taste-buds but a terrible waste of money, too.

Spices and Flavorings

From *The Bachelor Home Companion, 1987*

P. J. O'Rourke (1947–2022)

Salt keeps your blood pressure up to the pitch of modern life and improves all foods. Without salt, pretzels would be nothing but breadsticks with bad posture and potato chips would be potatoes. Use salt in everything.

(Incidentally, it's the salt in an olive that gives martini its snap. You can use a tiny pinch of table salt to make an emergency martini when you're out of olives and cocktail onions. Be careful, though. If you add too much salt, you'll wind up with a Margaritatini, which is awful.)

Pepper. Use everywhere you use salt, except the icy driveway.

Ketchup, The all-purpose flavor end-run. Should be used on anything that would be inedible if it didn't have ketchup on it.

Mustard is useful for cutting the excessively ketchupy taste so many foods have.

Sugar. Use anywhere salt doesn't seem to do the trick, e.g., in coffee and Kool-Aid, or on shredded wheat.

Lemon juice, an important ingredient in Bloody Marys and other forms of liquid breakfast. Makes fish taste as if it was grown on trees. And improves, immensely, the taste of lemons.

Wine splashes are vital when cooking for your date. A splash of wine turns anything into haute cuisine, at least early in a relationship. It looks as though you're making an effort.

Paradise

From *The Rubáiyát of Omar Khayyám, 1859*

Omar ibn Ibrahim al-Khayyám (1048–1131)

Translated by Edward FitzGerald (1809–1883)

XI

Here with a Loaf of Bread beneath the Bough,
A Flask of Wine, a Book of Verse – and Thou
    Beside me singing in the Wilderness –
And Wilderness is Paradise enow.

20 December

Futurist Formulas

From *The Futurist Cookbook, 1932*

Filippo Tommaso Marinetti (1876–1944) and Fillìa (Luigi Colombo, 1904–1936)

Translated by Suzanne Brill (1932–2020)

Like a Cloud
(formula by the futurist Aeropoet Guilio Onesti)
A great mound of whipped cream streaked with orange juice, mint,
strawberry jam and sprinkled lightly with Asti spumante.

Steel Chicken
(formula by the Futurist Aeropainter Diulgheroff)
Roast a chicken, emptied of its insides. As soon as it is cold, make an
opening in the back and fill the inside with red zabaglione on which
are laid two hundred grams of silver hundreds and thousands. Attach
cockscombs all round the opening.

Cosmic Apparitions
(formula by the Futurist Aeropainter Caviglioni)
Fennel, beetroot, turnips, yellow carrots on top of a spinach pie. Add
some candy floss. The boiled and buttered vegetables are cut in the
form of stars, moons, etc.

Surprise Bananas
(formula by the Futurist Piccinelli, cook at the Holy Palate)
Scoop out the cavity in a peeled banana and fill it with chopped
chicken meat.
Put it on the fire in a buttered pan and gradually add some meat
juices.
Serve with vegetables.

Indigestion and Drunkenness

From *The Physiology of Taste, 1825* |

Jean Anthelme Brillat-Savarin (1755–1826)

Translated by Fayette Robinson, 1854

Aphorisms of the Professor:

Those persons who suffer from indigestion, or who become drunk,
are utterly ignorant of the true principles of eating and drinking.

Presentation

From *The Constance Spry Cookery Book, 1956*

Constance Spry (1886–1960) and Rosemary Hume (1907–1984)

'It looked very nice but tasted of nothing.' 'It looked an awful mess but it didn't taste bad.' Is there a familiar note in either of those remarks? There is to me. If you are not interested in cooking you will hardly be reading this book; if you are I shall be forgiven if I take time here to write a little about the presentation of food.

First of all, I am sure we are all agreed that food should look pleasant, smell good, be harmonious to eye and palate. The appearance of the dish too, should indicate the nature of the food being offered. It may be permissible of the more frivolous reaches of the subject to make gingerbread look like unhealthy babies, a sponge cake depict a crinolined lady, or little cakes simulate apples or mushrooms, but such disguises are entirely out of place in the serious side of cooking. This does not mean that such food should not be decorative, only that it should be decorative in quite a different way; for example, a sole meunière with its brown buttery surface contrasting with the rich colour of the mushrooms, the rosiness of tomato and perhaps of orange is decorative, but it is not disguised, it is plainly fish; and since it looks and, we hope, smells and tastes good, it conforms to all the principles. Sole Colbert, too, with its contrast of golden crumbs and green butter, is another example, and so is a good cauliflower au gratin, milk-white, golden brown, with touches of tender green. I do hope I am making you feel hungry, for then all the points to be made will be half won.

A Ship, a Stag and a Castle

From *The Accomplisht Cook, 1660* | Robert May (1588–c1665)

Triumphs and Trophies in Cookery, to be used at Festival Times
Make the likeness of a Ship in Paste-board, with Flags and Streamers,
the Guns belonging to it of Kickses, bind them about with
packthread, and cover them with close paste proportionable to the
fashion of a Cannon with Carriages, lay them in places convenient as
you see them in Ships of war, with such holes and trains of powder
that they may all take Fire; Place your Ship firm in the great Charger;
then make a salt round about it, and stick therein egg-shells full of
sweet water, you may by a great Pin take all the meat out of the egg
by blowing, and then fill it up with the rose-water, then in another
Charger have the proportion of a Stag made of course paste, with a
broad Arrow in the side of him, and his body filled up with claret-
wine; in another Charger at the end of the Stag have the proportion
of a Castle with Battlements, Portcullices, Gates and Draw-Bridges
made of Past-board, the Guns and Kickses, and covered with course
paste as the former; place it at a distance from the ship to fire at
each other. The Stag being placed betwixt them with egg shells full
of sweet water (as before) placed in salt. At each side of the Charger
wherein is the Stag, place a Pye made of course paste, in one of which
let there be some live Frogs, in each other some live Birds; make these
Pyes of course Paste filled with bran, and yellowed over with saffron
or the yolks of eggs, guild them over in spots, as also the Stag, the
Ship, and Castle; bake them, and place them with guilt bay-leaves
on turrets and tunnels of the Castle and Pyes; being baked, make a
hole in the bottom of your pyes, take out the bran, put in your Frogs,
and Birds, and close up the holes with the same course paste, then
cut the Lids neatly up; To be taken off the Tunnels; being all placed

in order upon the Table, before you fire the trains of powder, order it so that some of the Ladies may be perswaded to pluck the Arrow out of the Stag, then will the Claret-wine follow, as blood that runneth out of a wound. This being done with admiration to the beholders, after some short pause, fire the train of the Castle, that the pieces all of one side may go off, then fire the Trains, of one side of the Ship as in a battel; next turn the Chargers; and by degrees fire the trains of each other side as before. This done to sweeten the stink of powder, let the Ladies take the egg-shells full of sweet waters and throw them at each other. All dangers being seemingly over, by this time you may suppose they will desire to see what is in the pyes; where lifting first the lid off one pye, out skip some Frogs, which make the Ladies to skip and shreek; next after the other pye, whence come out the Birds, who by a natural instinct flying in the light, will put out the Candles; so that what with the flying Birds and skipping Frogs, the one above, the other beneath, will cause much delight and pleasure to the whole company: at length the Candles are lighted, and a banquet brought in, the Musick sounds, and every one with much delight and content rehearses their actions in the former passages. These were formerly the delight of the Nobility, before good House-keeping had left *England*, and the Sword really acted that which was only counterfeited in such honest and laudable Exercises as these.

[The same is to be found in John Nott's *Cooks and Confectioners Dictionary*, 1723.]

The Turkey

From *A Christmas Carol, 1843* | Charles Dickens (1812–1870)

'It's Christmas Day!' said Scrooge to himself. 'I haven't missed it. The Spirits have done it all in one night. They can do anything they like. Of course they can. Of course they can. Hallo, my fine fellow!'

'Hallo!' returned the boy.

'Do you know the Poulterer's, in the next street but one, at the corner?' Scrooge inquired.

'I should hope I did,' replied the lad.

'An intelligent boy!' said Scrooge. 'A remarkable boy! Do you know whether they've sold the prize Turkey that was hanging up there? – Not the little prize Turkey: the big one?'

'What, the one as big as me?' returned the boy.

'What a delightful boy!' said Scrooge. 'It's a pleasure to talk to him. Yes, my buck!'

'It's hanging there now,' replied the boy.

'Is it?' said Scrooge. 'Go and buy it.'

'Walk-er!' exclaimed the boy.

'No, no,' said Scrooge, 'I am in earnest. Go and buy it, and tell 'em to bring it here, that I may give them the direction where to take it. Come back with the man, and I'll give you a shilling. Come back with him in less than five minutes and I'll give you half-a-crown!'

The boy was off like a shot. He must have had a steady hand at a trigger who could have got a shot off half so fast.

'I'll send it to Bob Cratchit's!' whispered Scrooge, rubbing his hands, and splitting with a laugh. 'He sha'n't know who sends it. It's twice the size of Tiny Tim.'

A Fat Brown Goose

From *The Dubliners: The Dead, 1914* | James Joyce (1882–1941)

A fat brown goose lay at one end of the table and at the other end, on a bed of creased paper strewn with sprigs of parsley, lay a great ham, stripped of its outer skin and peppered over with crust crumbs, a neat paper frill round its shin and beside this was a round of spiced beef. Between these rival ends ran parallel lines of side-dishes: two little minsters of jelly, red and yellow; a shallow dish full of blocks of blancmange and red jam, a large green leaf-shaped dish with a stalk-shaped handle, on which lay bunches of purple raisins and peeled almonds, a companion dish on which lay a solid rectangle of Smyrna figs, a dish of custard topped with grated nutmeg, a small bowl full of chocolates and sweets wrapped in gold and silver papers and a glass vase in which stood some tall celery stalks. In the centre of the table there stood, as sentries to a fruit-stand which upheld a pyramid of oranges and American apples, two squat old-fashioned decanters of cut glass, one containing port and the other dark sherry. On the closed square piano a pudding in a huge yellow dish lay in waiting and behind it were three squads of bottles of stout and ale and minerals, drawn up according to the colours of their uniforms, the first two black, with brown and red labels, the third and smallest squad white, with transverse green sashes.

Christmas Husbandlie Fare

From *Five Hundred Points of Good Husbandry, 1557, 1573*

Thomas Tusser (c. 1524–1580)

1. Good husband and huswife now cheefly be glad,
    things handsom to have, as they ought to be had;
They both doo provide against Christmas doo come,
    to welcome good neighbour, good cheere to have some.

2. Good bread and good drinke, a good fier in the hall,
    brawne, pudding and souse, and good mustard withall.

3. Beefe, mutton, and porke, shred pies of the best,
    pig, veale, goose and capon, and turkey well drest;
Cheese, apples and nuts, ioly Carols to heare,
    as then in the countrie is counted good cheare.

4. What cost to good husband is any of this?
    good houshold provision onely it is.
Of other the like, I doo leave out a menie,
    that costeth the husbandman neuer a penie.

A Merrycycle

From *Little Women, 1868* | Louisa May Alcott (1832–1888)

There never *was* such a Christmas dinner as they had that day. The fat turkey was a sight to behold, when Hannah sent him up, stuffed, browned, and decorated. So was the plum-pudding, which melted in one's mouth; likewise the jellies, in which Amy revelled like a fly in a honey-pot. Everything turned out well, which was a mercy, Hannah said, 'For my mind was that flustered, Mum, that it's a merrycle I didn't roast the pudding, and stuff the turkey with raisins, let alone bilin' of it in a cloth.'

Mr. Laurence and his grandson dined with them; also Mr. Brooke, – at whom Jo glowered darkly, to Laurie's infinite amusement. Two easy-chairs stood side by side at the head of the table, in which sat Beth and her father, feasting modestly on chicken and a little fruit. They drank healths, told stories, sang songs, 'reminisced', as the old folks say, and had a thoroughly good time. A sleigh ride had been planned, but the girls would not leave their father, so the guests departed early, and as twilight gathered, the happy family sat together round the fire.

Untraditional Christmas Food

From *Elizabeth David's Christmas, 2003* |

Elizabeth David (1913–1992)

If I had my way – and I shan't – my Christmas Day eating and drinking would consist of an omelette and cold ham and a nice bottle of wine at lunchtime, and a smoked salmon sandwich with a glass of champagne on a tray in bed in the evening. This lovely selfish anti-gorging, un-Christmas dream of hospitality, either given or taken, must be shared by thousands of women who know it's all Lombard Street to a China orange that they'll spend both Christmas Eve and Christmas morning peeling, chopping, mixing, boiling, roasting, steaming. That they will eat and drink too much, that someone will say the turkey isn't quite as good as last year, or discover that the rum for the pudding has been forgotten, that by the time lunch has been washed up and put away it'll be tea-time, not to say drink or dinner time, and tomorrow it's the weekend and it's all going to start all over again.

The Pudding

From *A Christmas Carol, 1843* | Charles Dickens (1812–1870)

Now, the plates being changed by Miss Belinda, Mrs. Cratchit left the room alone – too nervous to bear witnesses – to take the pudding up and bring it in.

Suppose it should not be done enough! Suppose it should break in turning out! Suppose somebody should have got over the wall of the back-yard, and stolen it, while they were merry with the goose – a supposition at which the two young Cratchits became livid! All sorts of horrors were supposed.

Hallo! A great deal of steam! The pudding was out of the copper. A smell like a washing-day! That was the cloth. A smell like an eating-house and a pastrycook's next door to each other, with a laundress's next door to that! That was the pudding! In half a minute Mrs. Cratchit entered – flushed, but smiling proudly – with the pudding, like a speckled cannon-ball, so hard and firm, blazing in half of half-a-quartern of ignited brandy, and bedight with Christmas holly stuck into the top.

Oh, a wonderful pudding! Bob Cratchit said, and calmly too, that he regarded it as the greatest success achieved by Mrs. Cratchit since their marriage. Mrs. Cratchit said that now the weight was off her mind, she would confess she had had her doubts about the quantity of flour. Everybody had something to say about it, but nobody said or thought it was at all a small pudding for a large family. It would have been flat heresy to do so. Any Cratchit would have blushed to hint at such a thing.

Today marks the end of the year and I feel one should start each new year with lists of things to look forward to, rather than lists of disheartening and unattainable aims. Here is a selection of my favourite food books, fact and fiction, which, for reasons of space or copyright, didn't fit in the anthology. These are books to read for inspiration, interest and entertainment; if I included all the recipe books I like I'd be here for ever.

Elizabeth David, Jane Grigson and Nigel Slater are in the anthology but they each earn a place here as it is their books I turn to most when I want culinary inspiration. I would recommend any and all of their writings.

Food Writing
Stewart Lee Allen, *In the Devil's Garden: A Sinful History of Forbidden Food*
Helena Atlee, *The Land Where Lemons Grow*
Raymond Blanc, *The Lost Orchard*
Lesley Blanch, *Round the World in Eighty Dishes*
Kate Colquhoun, *Taste*
Clarissa Dickson Wright, *A History of English Food*
Nicolas Freeling, *The Kitchen and The Cook*
Mark Kurlansky, *Milk*
Margaret Visser, *The Rituals of Dinner*
Michelle Zauner, *Crying in H Mart*

Books About Chefs and Cooks
Anthony Bourdain, *Kitchen Confidential*
Mary Contini, *Dear Francesca*
Julie Powell, *Julie & Julia: My Year of Cooking Dangerously*
Colette Rossant, *Apricots on the Nile*
Laura Shapiro, *What She Ate*
Stanley Tucci, *Taste*

Books to Dip Into

Larousse Gastronomique

Alan Davidson and Tom Jaine, *The Oxford Companion to Food*

Niki Segnit, *The Flavour Thesaurus*

Novels

Annabel Abbs, *The Language of Food*

Chitra Banerjee Divakaruni, *The Mistress of Spices*

Nora Ephron, *Heartburn*

Laura Esquivel, *Like Water for Chocolate*

Mary Essex, *Tea is So Intoxicating*

Patrick O'Brian, *Aubrey-Maturin* series

Children's Books

Enid Blyton, The Magic Faraway Tree series

René Goscinny and Albert Uderzo, Asterix series

Brian Jacques, Redwall series

Norton Juster, *The Phantom Tollbooth*

Noel Langley, *The Land of Green Ginger*

Arthur Ransome, Swallows and Amazons series

Index

Sources